SPOUSEWORK

SPOUSEWORK

✦

Partners Supporting Academic Leaders

Teresa Johnston Oden

iUniverse, Inc.

New York Lincoln Shanghai

SPOUSEWORK
Partners Supporting Academic Leaders

iUniverse books may be ordered through booksellers or by contacting:

iUniverse
2021 Pine Lake Road, Suite 100
Lincoln, NE 68512
www.iuniverse.com
1-800-Authors (1-800-288-4677)

Because of the dynamic nature of the Internet, any Web addresses or links contained in this book may have changed since publication and may no longer be valid.

The views expressed in this work are solely those of the author and do not necessarily reflect the views of the publisher, and the publisher hereby disclaims any responsibility for them.

ISBN: 978-0-595-45609-3 (pbk)
ISBN: 978-0-595-89910-4 (ebk)

Printed in the United States of America

For Rob, who helped me find the answers

Contents

Preface

This book is about being married to someone with a very particular kind of career, that of an academic leader. Whether the leader heads a boarding school or a college makes little difference. Over the past eighteen years my husband has done both.

In 1989 we took a leap. My husband gave up his position as a college professor and became headmaster of a boarding school, a move which some of his fellow professors considered tantamount to leaping into the void. In fact, the one who was leaping blindly was I. My husband had been in positions of leadership before; he had a good idea what he was in for. I did not.

Up to that point in our marriage, my life had not been impacted in any significant way by my husband's career. Before we made our decision to move to the boarding school, the search committee assured me that I would be free to do as much or as little as I liked. That was comforting. But since I was attracted to the idea of working closely with my husband in this position, I wanted to be actively involved as the headmaster's wife. Never mind that I had no prior exposure to boarding school life, that I had never even known a headmaster's wife.

Before we moved away to the boarding school, one of my co-workers teased me by saying, "So you are going to go and pour tea." I expected that spouses had long ago been excused from the tea table, and I certainly had not agreed to any such duty. But I didn't know how to respond to that jab, because I really had no idea what I would be doing. I looked for books that described the life of a leader's spouse, but those I found were written by an older generation and seemed untouched by the women's movement. I took that to mean that there wasn't much that the spouses of my day wanted to say. I should rather have assumed that those who had something they would have liked to say weren't talking.

Academic leaders, particularly those in charge of residential campuses, have jobs that overflow into their personal lives. They expect that this will happen. Their spouses expect that this will happen. Knowing that your life is going to be transformed, however, is not the same as knowing how you will react to that transformation. The first months after a new leader takes up his or her post can be a particularly challenging time for both leader and spouse. They step into a way of life that is fully formed, molded by forces outside the family circle. Odds are that it won't be a perfect fit for everyone. There is room for change, of course, but family needs must now be measured against institutional needs. The couple who doesn't come to grips with this fact is likely to be headed for trouble.

My personality was a poor fit for our new circumstances, and I expected to experience some distress as a result. But I am convinced that we were further hampered by a lack of information relating to the myriad ways our personal lives would be altered. Sorting out the tangle of complex, interlocking issues that affected our family was a long and lonely process. It took me years to figure out how to be the supportive partner I had hoped to be. That process would have been expedited, I believe, if I had had access to even one candid account of another spouse's experience. That is the chief reason I have written this book.

Most of us draw invisible lines around what we consider our private affairs. When you live in an official residence it isn't possible to draw such lines. This book reflects that situation. It is a hybrid, both the story of my personal journey insofar as that tale might help someone else, and a compendium of useful information that I picked up along the way. It is the sort of book I looked for but couldn't find when I stood on the brink of a new way of life and wondered just how dramatic the change might be. It is the sort of book I needed to read before we decided where to put the furniture in the official residence. It is the sort of book I could have turned to when I began to realize that the freedom I had been promised appeared to be hemmed in on all sides. I hope that it is the sort of book that would have reassured me when I was most discouraged, wondering if it wouldn't be better if I tuned out the noise of my husband's career and concentrated entirely on my own.

In writing this text I drew on my experiences but also on those of many others. As more women are appointed to leadership roles, the number of men in the spouse group grows. My discussions with some of these men have convinced me that, male or female, we spouses have many issues in common. However, the men among us have significant issues of their very own. At the end of each chapter I have appended a comment from one of the male spouses who shared their personal experiences with me.

Much that concerns the spouses of academic leaders also applies to those who partner leaders in other sectors: in government, the corporate world, the foreign service, the military and the ministry. I have addressed this book to the spouses, but the bulk of the material is relevant to the leaders themselves, whether they have partners or not. The final chapter is partially addressed to members of governing boards. Spouses want their partners to succeed; they are natural allies for governing boards. There are several ways boards could support these allies.

Readers who are merely curious are welcome. They will perhaps find that the lives that are lived behind the doors of an official residence are both less and more than they imagined.

Introduction

On the surface, there is only one thing we spouses have in common: we are partners of academic leaders. A mixed bag of men and women at different stages of our lives, with a variety of life experiences matched only by the variety of our personalities, we are at one remove from the group that can be expected to have a lot in common. If I were writing a book about rock collecting, I would despair if my publisher told me that the target audience was not the collectors, but the people who partner them. How would one write meaningfully for an audience made up of disparate individuals about whom one knows just this single fact, that they are all married to rock hounds?

Those of you who have already been initiated into the spouse corps will have quickly spotted the weakness in my analogy. If we were married to rock hounds, we might be able to ignore that fact and continue blithely on our own paths. But we can't do that, can we? *That* is what we have in common.

I suggest that we also share a particular goal. We want to be supportive. And this is what spousework is all about, supporting our leader-partners in an artful, intelligent way. How one manages to be a good spouse, in the context of partnering an academic leader, is not at all obvious. That's because spousework involves more than the two people who make the couple; it also involves the academy. A spouse can provide truly useful, truly intelligent support only after absorbing a considerable amount of information about, and understanding of, the institution that his or her partner leads.

When people ask me why I spend so much of my energy on spousework, considering that I don't have to, the first part of my answer is, "Because, like Everest, it is there." It's a challenge. And having at one time felt that the spouse's role had almost pinned me to the mat, it's a challenge I needed to face.

My decision to be actively involved as the spouse originated with a simple wish: to work closely with my husband toward a common goal. In those early days, if anyone had asked me what that common goal was, I probably would have said something like "the well-being of the school". Without a doubt, I was very, very naïve. I didn't foresee that this career change would flood every nook and cranny of our lives and that in response I would instinctively pull away. I had wanted to embrace this new life, but I was rattled by the abrupt loss of privacy and the sense that my husband's job was now controlling the whole family. I came to the conclusion that I had seriously misjudged myself; I was not going to be able to do even a decent job as the leader's spouse. I didn't want to change myself, even if I could; and I didn't think I could ever change the role enough to suit me.

However, there was no ignoring the elephant in our living room. There were ways in which I had to play the spouse, like it or not. So I picked out my path, trying to be a help-mate rather than a hindrance, second-guessing my actions, occasionally stepping on someone's toes. That period was painfully disconcerting for a woman who was more than forty years old and who had, for some time, seen herself as competent and able to handle all comers. I was repeatedly knocked off balance, sometimes at the very moment when my husband most needed a little support. And *I* had hoped to be a steadying anchor for *him*, when the going got rough!

At the end of our first year my husband and I were both utterly exhausted. We packed up, left campus and returned to our former home for a month of vacation. During those weeks I was able to take stock of our situation. My husband was obviously loving his new position, but the spouse's role, as I had experienced it that first year, was a serious disappointment to me. As a couple, we were thoroughly out of synch with each other, and that worried me. This job was working against us, and I had expected it to bring us closer together. How could I have been so wrong about that?

I couldn't figure out how to fix our problem, not at that early stage. But I could see that we, as a couple, were being challenged in a totally new way, and that I was the only one who could give priority to meeting that challenge. I slowly recognized that we had allowed a way of life to be imposed upon us. It was a way of life that might have suited another family perfectly well, but it wasn't going to work for us. If I had been more savvy and less starry-eyed starting out, perhaps I would have grasped much sooner that this was going to be the essence of my spousework: figuring out how to maintain some control over the way we lived from day to day, enough control so that the whole family would be comfortable in this new situation.

I had come with a humble attitude, knowing that I had to learn both about boarding-school life and about being the leader's wife. There are tales at many institutions about spouses who made a bad start by coming on too strong, and I was wary of that. But I had not apprehended the difference between a receptive stance and a passive one. I had been much too passive, and as a result I was in danger of becoming bitter and resentful.

In hindsight I can see how the solution to our problem evolved. I am dismayed to report that it took several years; it shouldn't have been, and needn't have been, so hard. I changed what I could, adjusted to what I couldn't change, and developed a certain attitude toward my husband's new career. That attitude may have been the most important element; it continues to serve me well each time a new situation arises and I must once again decide where to draw the line.

As my spelling checker keeps reminding me, spousework is not a word—so perhaps I need to provide a definition. I may have coined the term, but I didn't invent the pursuit. Spouses have been doing spousework for as long as people have had out-sized jobs that overflow onto their mates and into their personal lives. It is a way of life, comprising the thousand small adjustments one partner makes in order to facilitate, and cope with, the other partner's career. It is not unique to the academy. Couples in the corporate world, the foreign service, the military, the ministry and in government all recognize the need for spousework.

At the most fundamental level spousework is like an involuntary muscle. The heart muscle, if it is alive, *works*. Likewise, anyone who is partnering an academic leader is doing some spousework. It is a condition of that life. Like a heartbeat, we can participate in spousework at a resting rate, doing only as much as is inevitable, or we can ratchet up the extent of our involvement in our partners' careers and the life of the institution. Those of us who meet and greet our partners' constituents and take on tasks and responsibilities are simply exercising spousework at a different level.

Though spousework is something each of us must define for ourselves, the term can't help but call into the reader's mind another sort of occupation. There is only one word in common parlance which rhymes with "spousework". That fact begs the question whether I really intend to drag up the kind of baggage that goes with that other, homely word. Yes, dear reader, I do. Spousework can be hard, and there is not much glamour to it. Like housework, it's a job that seems to attract most notice when it is done badly, or not at all. Like housework, some elements of it may be, depending on one's personality, downright disagreeable. I'm not really suited to some parts of my role, even parts I've chosen to play. There's no surprise there; the institution didn't pick *me* out of an applicant pool. I believe that most of us spouses, no matter how carefully we tailor our roles, will end up with less than a perfect fit. But the same is true of life in general. The trick for us, we who design our spousework daily, is to find the positives that outweigh the negatives.

Constantly morphing and evolving with each day that passes, this is not a job of work that can be pinned down. There is no right or wrong way to do it, but all the same it can be done well, and it can be done poorly. Spousework to which you attach some value is spousework done well. My spousework has both a public and a private side. On the private side, I do whatever it takes to keep my husband's job from forcing unhappy, unhealthy compromises on us as a couple. I advocate for us as a family, serving as a sort of counterbalance to the institution, that entity whose needs constantly clamor for my husband's attention. On the public side I participate sufficiently in the life of the institution to feel a connection to it. Without that connection, my attitude toward my partner's career is affected. Without that public engagement, I tend to fall into resentment and bitterness, forgetting the privileges that attend this way of life and seeing only the trade-offs, the demands the institution makes on us separately and jointly.

Spousework looks like, to some degree *feels* like, a lop-sided pursuit. It becomes important, even necessary, only when one partner in a marriage takes a job that demands extraordinary commitment. Spousework matters when a person's career, by its very nature, insinuates itself into every aspect of what most of us consider to be our private affairs. It can become crucial to a marriage when one of the partner's professional responsibilities are so enormous that there is precious little time left to nurture personal relationships.

Let me be clear about what I mean. If my partner were simply a workaholic, I would not be so willing to help him in his career. That would amount to aiding and abetting him in what I consider to be a bad habit. Academic leaders—whether or not they are workaholics—hold offices that are peculiarly poised to consume the incumbent and wipe out personal relationships in the process. Put an over-achiever in charge of a residential campus, throw in a half-dozen constituencies with varying interests and needs, and you already have quite a stew—without even mentioning the real meat of the work, things like management decisions. An academic leader could easily fill every day and every evening of the week attending meetings or campus events, eating every meal with members of one or another of the many constituencies, and still find that some group feels it is being overlooked. It is that overload that makes it nearly impossible for a leader to devote time and energy to wondering how well his or her marriage is standing up to the pressure.

One of the first challenges I had to face as a spouse was the resentment that bloomed when my husband suddenly seemed absent from our relationship. It took a leap of faith at that point. I had to trust that he was not so enamored of his new position that I no longer mattered to him. Sometimes the job intruded in ways that made me wonder. Because spousework is inherently lopsided, I needed more than ever before to be sure that my partner was as committed to our relationship as I was. I was willing to meet him more than half-way, but I had to believe that he, too, was deeply committed to me.

Each spouse must, in the final analysis, find his or her own path through the maze. In my bleakest moments all those years ago I might have welcomed a book of advice that purported to be a foolproof guide for the spouse, that promised to tell me exactly what I needed to do to support my husband in his new career. Today I would wave off such a book. In the first place, there are too many variables between the spouses' individual situations. But more importantly, for every decision—even minor ones—that each of us is called upon to make, there are multiple factors which should be considered. Artful, intelligent spousework means, at base, knowing how to size up the couple's needs, individually and jointly, against the needs of the institution. The idea of a road map simply doesn't apply.

In this book I propose to describe the failures and successes, the thoughts and discoveries that comprise my education as the spouse of an academic leader. Perhaps my experience will help others see their own in a new light. Echoing Dante, I hope you will take what you can use and disregard the rest.

1

Preparing for a Different Way of Life

Will It Really Be So Different? In a word, the answer is "yes". When my husband switched from teaching at one institution to leading another, our lives changed abruptly and dramatically, and to my mind the only previous experience that was even worthy of comparison was the that of becoming parents some two decades earlier. There are many parallels in the two experiences. Parenthood is an event which people welcome into their lives, and then their first-born proceeds to turn their lives upside-down. Some changes are large and some are small; some are obvious and sudden, others are subtle, only slowly coming to light. It all happens in a soup of heightened feelings. Feelings of delight, concern, exhaustion and exhilaration come and go, in no particular order, during the baby's first weeks and months. It can be much the same for the couple embarking on a leadership position. The chief difference is that prospective parents generally have some idea what adjustments they will face, because they have seen others making the requisite changes.

When I finished the first draft of this book, I was surprised to see that this chapter, which is of the "Read this before you sign on the line" variety, was shaping up to be the longest one. Upon reflection I realized that I could have predicted this. When I was new, I was new three times over: in an unfamiliar role, in an alien academic environment, in a strange town. All told, I was practically moving to a foreign country. There was little in my introverted, seclusion-loving personality that was going to make me a "natural" in this role; I had some inkling about that even before I understood much about being a headmaster's wife. Also, I had decided that I would not look for a job outside the home. This seemed wise, considering all the changes that my husband and I, and the one child still living at home, would be facing. There's no doubt, however, that it added to the load of emotional adjustment I had to make.

As I dredged up my memories of my first year partnering an academic leader, it became clear that any discourse I wrote on this topic might serve rather to discourage than support others who find themselves in the spouse role. Much of the early *sturm und drang* I experienced as the spouse had to do with my lack of experience with leadership roles, and with my psychological make-up—that of an introvert with a need for privacy that borders on the morbid. I hope the reader will try to keep this in mind. It seems to me that it would become tedious if I constantly threw out reminders that my experience was, in several ways, a worst-case scenario.

We began in a state of head-spinning busy-ness and excitement which I suspect is pretty common among couples making this kind of change. I assumed that it would mostly be a matter of time for us to adjust to living in the middle of a campus and in a new town. As for my role as the school head's spouse, I intended to wait and see how I might want to be involved. It seems to me now that this was a very passive attitude. But how could it have been otherwise? In the spring before our move I was preparing to leave my old job and move our household; my husband was still teaching his college classes and, at the same time, becoming heavily involved in boarding school matters. There was no time for either of us to sit and wonder what we were getting ourselves into. There was no book for me to read that might have offered a peek into our future.

In retrospect I can describe what sort of attitude might have been appropriate. Again, parenthood provides a fine analogy. For an expectant parent, even the one who is to be the secondary parent and therefore less involved in the actual care of the infant, a "wait and see" attitude is a little too casual. Most of us brace ourselves mentally, even though we can't really know what we are in for. We expect that we are going to have to make space in our lives for new demands. We wonder how we will cope if something goes wrong. We wait and see, but with apprehension. There's always a chance that it's going to be much harder work than we anticipated, that our experience won't be like those glowing television commercials which show the new parents bringing the baby home from the hospital.

The analogy holds up beyond the period of anticipation. There is no gradual phasing-in of parenthood. Once that baby comes home, there you are—responsible for feeding, diapering, comforting, bathing, all these things you've never dealt with before. You learn by doing. New parents foul up, realize it and change tactics. Thank goodness the baby is too young to know that the parents are fumbling.

Likewise a new leader—or his or her spouse—occasionally fouls up, realizes it and changes tactics. People may see what looks like a false step, but they hold off judgment for a while as the new administration gets underway. You get a grace period. I wish that, in those first months, I had cards with those words taped around the house.

Here's a little story that conveys what it can feel like to be the spouse, fumbling about with a new role.

My wife was the new president, and we had moved into the president's house just a few weeks before. We were hosting our first party, for an alumni group. I was mixing with the guests in the living room when a man nodded toward the fireplace and said, "I see you've removed the portrait that used to hang there."

I knew instantly that I was in a minefield. It didn't seem wise to just tell him the truth, that we didn't care for that portrait. Was this guy an art expert? Did his family give that painting to the institution? I could admit that I didn't like it much—you know, making it clear that my wife had nothing to do with the decision. I was thinking as fast as I could while starting to answer him with a long, slow, "Yessss ..." I didn't want to seem too curt or unfriendly. I had to say something more. Before I knew it I was blurting out, "Actually, it frightened our children." What an idiot thing to say! I worried all evening that my wife may have given someone else a different answer. To top it all off, our kids aren't that young. If the word got around this community, people would think we're making babies of them!

This person wants to be a supportive spouse but he's a bit at sea. He realizes that he has been thrust into a world where everything he does can have ramifications, where anything he says might come back to bite him. He is beginning to see ways in which he might be a liability for his partner. He's not sure he has the information he needs to do a decent job. You might judge him to be a fool and think that you could never be reduced to such a state. But I can tell you, it happens. The stress and fatigue of moving into the new position, combined with days and weeks of meeting dozens, if not hundreds, of new people, take a toll. You become weary, physically, emotionally, and even socially—so weary that your self-confidence may seep away. Sure, this guy is a little overwrought; he probably isn't sleeping well and is walking around in a fog. He is temporarily overwhelmed by the change all around him. What's worse is that he didn't see it coming. That's pretty disconcerting for someone who is used to feeling in full command of himself.

Being Supportive: The New Challenge. I'm sure I am not the only "seasoned" spouse who feels that, during the first years after my partner's career change, I did a rather lousy job when it came to providing support. Certainly I tried to be sensitive to my husband's needs; I tried to be understanding and loyal. That was the role of supportive spouse as I had understood it up to that point in our marriage. The problem was that my husband's new job was so much more complex than what he had done before that the old concept, though it still applied, fell way short, and I had not yet analyzed this incongruity. For years my partner had been building the skills he would need in this new career. It seemed to me that his appointment to a leadership post was the logical next step in what had been a steady progression. And I expected that I would, as before, just bounce up and stand beside him. It never occurred to me that we had reached a level where I would suddenly find obstacles in my way as I prepared to step up and claim my accustomed place.

I assumed that I was fully competent to make this move, when in fact I was like a child learning to talk, picking up the language from the environment, absorbing the rules of grammar without being aware of it. In the beginning my support skills were not up to the demand for them. When we hit a rough patch, some sort of crisis on campus, I tried to be reassuring, but my own emotional responses were hardly helpful. When my husband was really worried, I got scared. (He had given up tenure for a career where the incumbents lasted, on average, about four years!) When he was nearly overwhelmed by problems or by the demands of his schedule, I felt angry about all the stress he had to deal with. I was terribly lonely. All I had wanted to do was help my partner bear his load, but I was probably making it heavier. It was hard to disguise my distress.

In those early days I was supporting my husband in several ways—mechanically (taking on some of the tasks and duties he could delegate to me without raising any eyebrows) and spiritually (being an ally, offering encouragement). But something was missing: I did not know how to support him *intelligently*. I was a spectator on the sidelines, cheering on my favorite player without any real understanding of the rules of the game. I might as well have been watching the movement of colored pieces in a kaleidoscope. It was impossible for me to see a move or two ahead, to predict what consequences might follow certain actions. Living life that way was extremely wearing. What a relief, then, when I began to comprehend patterns and know what to expect. At the same time I was gradually coming to recognize and appreciate the particular skills my husband was using to meet the challenges he faced. In this process I was actually acquiring the skills *I* needed to be supportive in the fullest sense. Without those skills I was not able to use my eyes and ears to gather fresh information. Nor was I worth much as a sounding board. With them I would on occasion make a truly useful suggestion. Working with my partner in this way was so gratifying that I realized I might, after all, get as much out of spousework as I was putting into it.

To be a supportive spouse in an intelligent way you need a good understanding of the personalities, politics and problems that are shaping the institution from day to day. You need to know something about the history of the place. You need to be able to think politically, not with cunning but with wariness. You need a good understanding of your partner's role and what parts of it are hardest for him or her.

Some spouses will come to the role already prepared to give intelligent support. Others will have to work as I did, if they want to break through to this level. Once you are there, you can offer valuable ideas and insights. The two of you can truly be a team, helping each other out with the most vital issues. Supporting my husband intelligently is for me the best, most rewarding part of spousework.

There is so much more to say about this subject, but it belongs in another chapter. For now I just want to make this point. Spousework can be much more than fending off the monster-job that will gobble up your marriage if you let it. I didn't always think this was so.

Developing a Relationship with the Board. In common practice the incoming spouse has little, if any, relationship with the search committee. There is generally not much improvement when the search committee passes off its charge and the board steps in. A new leader's relationship with the institution's board of trustees is crucial to his or her success. And yet many boards seem to studiously avoid even the beginning of an official relationship with the leader's spouse. I think that, in this respect, boards are missing an opportunity. The spouse is someone who could be a natural, and strong, ally. Like the board, the spouse wants to see the new leader succeed and is most likely willing to go some distance to help that happen.

It is not hard to come up with one very good reason why search committees and boards are tiptoeing around the spouses these days; Affirmative Action legislation altered everything. But that is only the beginning of the awkwardness. These entities cannot know how to begin to deal with you until they know you as a person. Are you someone who would like to be included in the interview process, who feels you definitely should be included at the interview stage, or who feels that that would be entirely inappropriate? How can they find out without interviewing you? You see the problem. Neither the search committee nor the board wants the spouse to feel ignored. Yet if they seem too attentive that might give rise to false hopes—or fears. In all likelihood, few members of the search committee or the board have prior experience when it comes to choosing a leader for the campus. They are learning as they go. I think it's safe for us spouses to assume that, before our partners are given the nod, there's been some wrangling behind closed doors over the question of the proper treatment of the leader's spouse.

We can take some initiative here by making certain our partners know where we stand on some of the questions that are sure to arise. We can (and should in any case) discuss with our partners ahead of time how we feel about maintaining our own careers, traveling with the leader, accepting pay if offered, and taking on tasks which have traditionally been handled by the (traditionally female) spouse. Our partners can plug this information into discussions with the search committee or the board, if and when it seems appropriate. Ideally these discussions would begin when the search committee has selected its shortlist, but before any final deal is done.

I am guessing that most boards of trustees meet the spouse for the first time at just this point, when the shortlist is formulated; this has certainly been true for me. My first meetings have varied from a dinner meeting where I moved from table to table during the meal—a quite casual just-getting-to-know-you scenario (or so it seemed)—to a joint interview with my husband, during which I sensed that the questions the board directed to me had been well thought out ahead of time.

Once the board has acknowledged the existence of a spouse (by meeting him or her), it is time in my opinion for both parties to become more open about their hopes, aims and expectations. It is time for the spouse to start asking a lot of questions. It is time to tour the official residence, if that is where you would be expected to live. It is time to learn about budgets and support staff. The window of opportunity here is very small, I realize, and may be missed altogether. But better late than never. If your partner has already accepted the job offer, but you have not yet moved in, that's still a decent time for these exchanges.

Establishing Your Own Identity. There are two issues involving the spouse's identity. First there's the need that anyone feels when moving to a new community. You would like to give people some sense of who you are. A related issue is the need to let people know how you differ from the previous incumbent's spouse (if there was one) or from anyone else they have ever known who shared a similar role. I will start with the second issue, which is somewhat simpler to treat.

When the search committee told me I would be free to do as much or as little as I liked, I accepted their assurances in good faith. I am sure they were given in good faith. Only much later did I begin to wonder just how members of the various constituencies—alumni, students, their parents, and so on—would know that the institution and I had struck a deal. Indeed, I don't believe that would be possible. There was no reason that the community should expect me to behave any differently from my predecessor. For all anyone knew, we had both signed up to stand in receiving lines, join certain community organizations and eat meals with students from time to time.

How does one counteract this tendency? I think it's a good idea to learn as much as possible about what exactly your predecessor did, in the way of spouse-work, and the more detail the better. In what events did he or she participate? Who were the closest and most frequent contacts within the campus community? What sort of visible civic involvement did he or she have? In short, find out what folks have been conditioned to expect. It is the best way to avoid being taken by surprise.

For both the leader and the spouse who are new to a campus, expectations surface in dozens of little ways during the first months and years. Even when you've done your research you may be caught short once in a while. It is hard to credit the fact that expectations might touch on what many of us consider our most private affairs. On a campus that had no strong connection with any established religion, my husband and I were surprised when we were pressured to worship in a particular church, because our predecessors had been members of that congregation.

When I have the feeling that someone with whom I am getting acquainted has certain expectations of me, I drop a comment or two into the conversation, indicating in so many words that I am actively involved in figuring out just how I am going to be involved, and that that is going to take some time. It is very easy to find yourself "volunteered" for a lot of different efforts, and very hard to extricate yourself gracefully when you discover you don't have time or aren't really interested. Even the most forward people have taken the gentle hints I've dispensed. Most folks just need to be nudged toward the realization that you and your predecessor are two distinct people who might make different choices. And, perhaps, they need to be awakened to the fact that some of these things *are* choices and not inescapable parts of every spouse's role today.

The second identity issue, establishing oneself as an individual with a full-fledged personality, takes time and patience. In the search process the primary focus is naturally on the leadership candidates. Their personalities and personal histories have been thoroughly probed. The spouses, on the other hand, remain shadowy characters till the end, or nearly the end, of the process. You may arrive on campus together, but one of you will be a known entity and the other will be a mystery person.

The terms "leading spouse" and "trailing spouse" are much in vogue these days, whenever the topic of discussion is two-career marriages where one of the careers is taking a back seat. These terms, suggesting as they do two people in some kind of foot race with each other, are most unfortunate. I wish I could appropriate them for a different use, to describe an incoming leader and his or her partner. Those of us who go along with our mates when they take leadership positions are often "trailing"—not in our careers, but in identity recognition. Campus and city newspapers have printed biographical sketches of the new leader; articles have appeared in publications sent to alumni and other campus stakeholders. But little information has been distributed about the spouse. He or she might appear in a photograph or two, and may be mentioned at the end of the biography, identified as a "teacher", "homemaker", "lawyer". Generally, that's about it.

This low-profile introduction to the community is appropriate, but at the same time, people really expect to see you sharing the spotlight when the leader is introduced in a social setting. There's liable to be some consternation if you continually fail to make an appearance; your absence will be noted. It's a bit strange to be suddenly thrust into the spotlight, after you've been kept in the dark during much of the search process.

Establishing your identity as a person, separate from your partner, is one of the biggest issues for many spouses, especially when the couple is settling into a new community, and this is where it all begins. Some of us go through a mini identity crisis at this point. We've removed ourselves from those who knew us before, and parked ourselves among people who will always see us, first and foremost, as "the spouse". We would like to be appreciated for our own special talents and accomplishments; everyone likes to feel appreciated! But at this very point in time we may not exactly be at our best. This is one of the sneakiest things about the adjustments one is called upon to make. For most of us they come at a time in mid-life when we know ourselves pretty well, when we are comfortable with ourselves and confident that we can cope. We want others to see us as individuals instead of dismissing us with a quick nod, and yet, perversely, we may be in a state of flux, living with more self-doubt than we've had for a long time. I have huge admiration for anyone who can get through this without feeling the least bit shaken!

It is easy in the first days and months to feel invisible, even though you are in all likelihood more visible in the literal sense than you've ever been before. You are included at social events, and people line up to meet you, but there can be a hollowness in all this. You might come to feel like a figurehead or a proxy, widely recognized but not for any special talent of your own. You are the trailing spouse, but only temporarily. The situation improves over time, as people on campus, in the community, and perhaps in a new workplace come to appreciate you as an individual. It's not going to happen in the first stage, in those huge "getting to know you" gatherings, where you stand in receiving lines for hours. It will probably begin with one person at a time, perhaps as you sit down and converse with a dinner partner. It is a slow and frustrating process, but things will right themselves in the end.

The most hurtful thing to me, ironically, is the feeling that I'm not even recognized as a figurehead. When people brush right past me, as I stand next to my husband dutifully greeting guests, it's hard not to conclude that they are simply rude. The rudeness may be unintentional, but there it is. And this, unfortunately, continues to happen, since every year brings to campus its quota of new students and parents, and less-active alumni, whom we have never met before—people who may have heard my husband speak or seen his photo but who couldn't pick me out of a crowd. I try to remember that the point of these folks' visit is not to meet the spouse—that sometimes they are not much interested in meeting the leader, either. They are pre-occupied with other matters—I will grant them that.

I still spend many hours standing in receiving lines each year, but fewer than I used to. When we entertain in our home, I often move around the reception, while my husband stands near the door so that he can greet every guest. I don't meet every guest this way, but I can make real connections with the people I do meet. I can also scan for people who are standing apart, perhaps because they don't know anyone; I can facilitate introductions to other guests. I am sure that I did not have the confidence to do this in the very beginning, being shy by nature and, temporarily, confidence-challenged. It's a habit that developed naturally, when I started to realize that I was more comfortable working a party this way than standing by my husband as his mute sidekick. In other situations I have been more pro-active. If a situation is irksome because I find myself cast too obviously in the role of figurehead, I might make a suggestion that we do it differently next time.

There is no salve for general invisibility, but I find I can cope with that as long as my husband recognizes and appreciates my efforts. I believe it is vitally important for our partners to have a good understanding of what it is like for us, and this can only happen with hours and hours of talking about it. After many discussions over the years, my husband knows what parts of the role I play are the most uncomfortable for me, and he is empathetic. He expresses his appreciation often, and I need for him to do that.

Keeping a Low Profile. There was a time when our society felt that children should be "seen but not heard". These days we smile on children who behave in ways that would have been considered rambunctious in the past; we allow them much more leeway in expressing themselves. Unfortunately, leaders' spouses are still, as a class, subject to something very like that old rule. Particularly in the early days of a new leader's tenure, we spouses are expected to be visible. We are expected to be visible because that shows that we understand the seriousness of the leader's role and are ready to lend support. But we are not expected to say much of anything. Indeed, if we are too verbose, too revealing, it might cause consternation in one quarter or another.

I'm sorry to have to say it, but, in my opinion, the wise spouse will stay pretty quiet, for a while at least. When a new leader takes over, people are searching for any information that will give them insight into the new administrator *qua* administrator. As the spouse, you are likely to meet people who will consider you to be a spokesperson for your partner. If you express an opinion, these folks will take it to be your partner's considered opinion. Even worse, people may infer something about the administrator's personality based on interactions with the spouse. If the spouse is perceived as opinionated and hard-edged, or flighty and bubbleheaded—I exaggerate, you understand, in order to make my point—the new leader may have to work overtime to reassure constituents that he or she is not cut from the same cloth.

Unfair? Absolutely. The good news is that this is more of a problem at the start, and perhaps only at smaller institutions. I hated to think it was a problem even then, but I decided to bow to a hint from a more experienced spouse. In our first year my husband and I attended a conference for school heads, and I joined a session organized for spouses. We were asked to choose a topic from a short list and gather with others who wished to discuss that topic. I chose the topic "Being New". A woman in this group indicated that she really didn't want to make trouble for her husband, but she was pretty impatient with the need to never express an opinion about anything of real substance, for fear that listeners would assume they were hearing the leader's opinion. There were knowing nods around the circle. I seemed to be the only one who was at all startled by this comment. I wasn't about to leave it there; this was 1990, after all! So I said, "Surely you could make it clear that it was your own personal opinion, and not that of your partner." "Oh, no," she replied. "I *could* do that, but if I did there would be rumors flying around that our marriage was in trouble." I may have been rather green yet, but I had lived on a small campus long enough to recognize the truth of that statement. I didn't want speculation of that type in the air, so I took her advice to heart. As I say, I think this is an issue mostly in the early days. Once you are known, as individuals and as a couple, once your united front is recognized, you can perhaps admit that you plan to cancel out your mate's vote in the next presidential election.

And consider this: your partner will also be squelching some part of his or her individuality. Rita Bornstein, long-seasoned as a college president herself, has written about the conflict academic leaders feel as they begin to play down their "authentic" selves in order to better represent their institutions' interests (see "The Authentic, and Effective, College President", *The Chronicle of Higher Education*, July 30, 2004). This is but one of many ways that the two of you will be sharing the experience of academic leadership when you are with the public. And when you are alone together, that is when both of you can revert to your natural selves.

Preparing Others for Change. This subhead is meant, I suppose, to be provoking. It may seem rather bold and presumptuous for the leader's spouse to be thinking about ways other people are going to have to change *their* roles. But there is a valid point to be made. If your spousework is going to extend into task-sharing with your partner, by planning the entertaining or caring for an official residence, for example, you need to have some clear authority. You are not being presumptuous if your partner is willing to share with you the responsibility and authority for these things. However, if you *are* going to be task-sharing, then your partner needs somehow to get the message out that you are the one who is in charge of certain matters, that your requests for help should be attended to as though they came from the top. It is not hard for the president or school head to send this message. "My wife will handle your questions about renovating the residence" or "My husband will work with you in planning this event"—a directive of that type may be all that is needed.

The appointment of a new leader implies change. Depending on the circumstances at your institution, people may be positively looking forward to some sort of change. And yet, change is never an easy matter. The prospect makes some people very nervous; the implementation may leave them feeling threatened. The changes that you, the spouse, might want to make are probably going to be less central to campus life than the ones your partner is going to make, but that does not mean that no one is going to be upset by them.

It is good to keep people mindful of the possibility of change, even if you are not ready to start moving things around. Those who might be anxious about alterations coming along in the future can be lulled into a false sense of security when they see the *status quo* going forward for a time.

My task-sharing has included overseeing the official residence and any functions that we host there. My husband and I assumed that it would take a while for us to recognize what we needed to change in these matters, or what we wanted to change to suit us better. At each new post, we started out our first year carrying on pretty much as our predecessors had. We were busy enough just moving in, meeting people and getting the year rolling. The academic calendar determined much of our entertaining, and that had been set long before. We did a little remodeling and redecorating, but anything that was very disruptive waited until after the autumn rush of events was past. And in the first months, as I casually mentioned now and then that we would eventually have furniture in the living room, I tried also to keep people mindful that we might, in due course, alter other things as well.

One thing that didn't seem odd when my husband took up his new career all those years ago, now seems to me to be a very peculiar practice: passing along the housekeeper together with the house keys. Our first residence was enormous, with bedrooms numbering in the double digits. We ran a sort of bed and breakfast, putting up many school guests. We easily kept a housekeeper busy for thirty hours each week. I knew I needed this person's help, and a sense of gratitude was foremost in my mind. As it happened, the whole family developed a good relationship with the housekeeper. But what if we hadn't liked her? What if we hadn't felt we could trust her? And what if she hadn't liked us? I don't think anyone considered these possibilities. I know cases where such things have happened, and it has been an awful mess for all concerned. In several cases the unhappy situation went on for years.

In this matter academic institutions might well take a page from the corporate world. No one is much surprised when a new CEO appoints different people to some of the organization's top positions. The leader values this freedom to choose those with whom he or she will work most closely. I believe that a family moving into the official residence should be given similar freedom to replace those who will be working in and around their home. It is *at least* as important on the home front as in the office place.

Unfortunately, the institution may overlook the issue of staffing at the residence as everyone scurries about preparing for the transition. This is a potentially serious oversight. It would be wise for the department of human resources to meet with anyone who regularly works a significant number of hours in or around the residence and introduce them to the idea of possible changes in the future. Domestic staff need to understand that the new residents will be looking for a good fit—people who will suit them well, in a very personal way—and that no blame will attach to either side if the fit between the family and an existing staff member turns out to be poor. The employees need to know that, whatever happens, the institution will look out for them. And they need to know that, whatever happens, the new residents will be eternally grateful for their help in coping with things during the early days.

Your "passed along" staff may be wonderful; you may not want to change anything at all. Still, it will not hurt for them to have the idea that the new residents will be taking a wait-and-see approach to continuing their services. We have all had the experience of a relationship starting well but turning sour, whether it was with a room-mate, co-worker or friend. There are things that you simply can't know at the start, no matter how positive the signs.

Advice *Will* Be Given—but Beware! As a novice spouse I often took the advice of those around me who were more familiar with the institution, but an experience early on taught me to be very cautious about accepting advice without carefully examining it. The counsel I took, but lived to regret, involved restricting a guest list for an annual party that was on the verge of being too large to handle. It came mixed with other advice that seemed sound enough, so I didn't question it. When this particular party came around, I struck the retired faculty from the guest list. It was a bad decision. As it turned out, the advice I was given might have been good ten years before, when the retired faculty as a group were very elderly and reluctant to attend large parties. But in *my* time the group of retirees included a number of people who were still vitally active and who prized this annual chance to mix with their former colleagues. I hurt a lot of feelings.

And so I warn my readers, please pick and choose among the bits of advice that I dole out. I intend them more as possibilities for your consideration than a recipe for success!

Each time we moved to a different institution, I was glad there were so many employees who were content to simply carry on as they used to, with little guidance. But this is truly a double-edged sword. "We've always done it this way" can be a help at first, but it can also become a hindrance ere long.

During one transition I was truly blessed to work closely with an employee who seemed to be exquisitely sensitive to our situation. As we worked together on entertainment plans she made it clear to me that she was happy to tell me how things had been done in the past, if I wanted to know, but she had no expectations that my husband and I would want to do things the same way. This was, to my mind, the ideal attitude.

Finding Support. If we are playing the role of supportive spouse, we surely have the right to expect that we, in turn, will get some support from our partners. But I think it would be unfair to expect to get all the support we need from this source. Family members and old friends will surely be sympathetic, but often they are not able to comprehend the many ways your life has changed, and the support they give may be off target. I have found the most meaningful support among other spouses.

The spouses of leaders at institutions similar to yours are the only people who can even begin to understand what you are experiencing. I was lucky indeed to find a group of spouses waiting to welcome me when my husband became a headmaster. The academic year had barely begun, but I was already full to bursting with things I wanted to tell someone—things I knew instinctively would not sit well with anybody I'd met so far. Things like the fact that we weren't finding the headmaster's house, which was large and elegant and beautifully decorated, all that easy to live in. I was feeling very insecure as a result of the rapidity of change, and I badly needed some reassurance that I was doing okay, that I was still the competent adult I had thought myself to be as recently as a few months before. I was really looking forward to meeting with the support group.

My initial meeting with the group was memorable. As we gathered at a restaurant that noon, one woman plopped down into a chair and started in on a story. "You won't believe," she began in an exasperated tone, when the woman who had organized this particular gathering interrupted. "Oh, I was so hoping that we wouldn't all *complain* today." She was perhaps feeling the hostess' burden and wanted to welcome (and not scare) me, the newest member of the group. Perhaps she was a bit surprised that I was the first to respond to her plea, with a somewhat anguished, "Oh, but that's just what I was hoping we *would* do!" I laughed when I realized what I had said, and so did everyone else. We had a wonderful time together.

There is such a thing as a valid complaint, and it helps when we express it to someone who can truly understand and sympathize. We all need to be free to complain once in a while; the problem for us as spouses is to find a safe place in which to do it. I in no way mean to suggest that we all should arrange for whine-fests; I think one can draw a line between whining and complaining. A child with a newly-skinned knee has a valid complaint; if that child is still trying to get sympathy for the knee two weeks later, that's whining. The real issue lies elsewhere, and whining is fruitless in the long run.

I have no idea how many localized support groups are out there; I hope the number is growing. When I didn't find such a group after one of our moves, I organized one. I quickly found three people who leapt at the chance to meet this way.

Friends Old and New. One of the paradoxes of my partner's position is that, while we have more friends than ever before, almost none of the friendships is close. The welcome given to a new leader, and his or her spouse if there is one, is exuberant and warm; most of us haven't experienced anything like it since we were newborns. But these welcoming folks are nearly all destined to be what I call "friends of office". Friends of office are like those new shoes whose leather is just a tad too thick and stiff: they are never going to feel like the old, comfortable ones they replaced. The common bond with all these new acquaintances is the institution, and the institution will always be in the way.

It is quite natural to look to old friends for that comfortable feeling, but many times old friendships have to be re-examined when your partner moves into a leadership position. You may have a dear friend who could be a wonderful source of support—except that he or she just talks too much and lives too near. I know that in the beginning I let myself, more than once, be rather indiscreet while talking with an old friend I'd moved away from. Just in case, I was always careful to specify, "This is between you and me." One day I realized that such confidences could easily amount to burdens. Why should my friends have to remember what part of our conversation was to be kept confidential? I was learning (as I explicate more fully in the chapter on information) that decisions which seemed to me to be of almost no consequence were nonetheless potentially painful for someone, and that it was best for me to avoid discussion of them. It seemed positively unfair to expect my old friends to understand such things, to remember to keep something confidential when it wasn't at all obvious why that should matter.

My husband has always moved into his leadership positions from outside the campus. I suspect someone could write a chapter, if not a book, about what it is like to move into the leadership of an institution with which you have a long-standing connection. I have not had that experience, but I will bet that dealing with old friendships within the campus community is one of the most delicate issues, for both the leader and the spouse. For me, always coming from the outside, the delicate issue has been how to deal with someone who clearly wants to be my new friend. I am sure that the mixture of warmth and coolness that people sense from me in these situations is puzzling for them. While I seem pleased by chance meetings, I never initiate any activities and seldom make even a phone call. Occasionally I discover that the individual was close friends with the previous incumbent, and then I can't help but wonder whether he or she is driven primarily by the hope of once again being part of an inner circle. I understand that desire; I treasure my own place in that inner circle.

I sometimes encounter people who share my interests to such an extent that I know we could be wonderful friends, if only the circumstances were different. I enjoy the hours I spend with friends of office, but for these years, my husband has to be my best and closest friend. I am content with that.

Designing a Getaway. I don't recall that we had a true break from life on campus, or campus concerns, during our first year, but things probably would have gone better with us if we had. Our vacation at the end of the year was the best we could have designed, but it happened purely by chance, shaped by events beyond our control. We had not had time to sell the house we had been living in before my husband took this new job, so we rented it out for the academic year and planned to return to it the next summer. One month back in that old home taught us that that was just the vacation we needed. The weight of campus worries fell away when we dropped back into our former, simple and familiar life for a few weeks. Away from the campus, we got some perspective on the year that had passed. We recognized that regular breaks were no luxury but rather were going to be absolutely essential.

During the hustle of the first year, and every year thereafter, it can be hard to make time to even plan a break for yourselves, much less take one. It really doesn't matter what you do; time to yourself is the key. Block some out as soon as you can, and then be fierce about protecting it through the months ahead.

From a Male's Point of View: "[A male] will be considered odd (weak, underachieving, etc.) as a spouse unless you transport a career with you. If you don't move with her, though, you will be considered a selfish cad who doesn't support his wife, and rumors of divorce will beat you to campus."

2

Looking Over the House that Comes with the Job

House or Mausoleum? Look at that lovely, old home, so elegant, so enormous, surrounded by its beautiful grounds, so conveniently located for all the campus guests who come and go. What a grand tradition it is for institutions to house their leaders in such style! Right? Well, hold on. Sometimes it's a case of big house, big headache.

Our first residence was so impressive, we were bowled over. We felt like we had arrived. My husband's new job was going to be demanding, we knew, and this abode was part of the reward for all that hard work. There was so much space that the old servants' quarters alone would have made a modest home. I will never forget the gleeful cry of one of our daughter's friends when she first saw the headmaster's house. Standing at the railing in the dining room, looking over the sunken living room and the adjacent music room with its two grand pianos, Fern cried, "Kate, you live in a castle!" There were so many bathrooms, my husband and I decided we would designate one "His" and another "Hers". There were fireplaces in most of the bedrooms. It was beautifully decorated. We were dazzled, and we did not reflect very carefully on this place that was to become our home. It had been the headmaster's house for a century. Surely the kinks had been worked out!

Within a few months we were beginning to recognize the issues. Location was a big one. The house faced a small quadrangle, with the chapel and two dormitories forming the other three sides. Students and faculty passed by throughout the day and evening, their voices ricocheting off the nearby brick buildings, continually fooling us into thinking people were conversing on our front porch. For us on the inside, the only way to go from the kitchen to the second floor, where the bedrooms and the family room were located, was to use the grand central staircase which was in full view from the windows on either side of the front door.

17

My husband and I had both been trapped in the kitchen in our pajamas when someone arrived unexpectedly and rang the bell. We soon learned to keep the ground floor in near darkness in the evening so that we could not be so easily observed as we moved about.

Since there were five or six bedrooms we couldn't possibly need for our own use, we weren't surprised to be told that we would be expected to house school guests. Guests were welcome to dine at the cafeteria, and the housekeeper would take care of their rooms. No problem, or so we thought. We did not fully comprehend what was being asked of us. I now realize that the search committee and the board of trustees probably understood as little as we did. (Indeed, the search committees and boards of trustees at all of the institutions we have served were knowledgeable about life on campus but knew next to nothing about life in an official residence.) Only after we moved in did we learn that "guests" might, for example, mean a whole troupe of actors, settling in for a week, leaving behind red-wine stains on the bedroom carpets. We must be grateful, I suppose, that they did not take their jugs of wine, stopped up with rags, into the school dining room.

We knew we would be living in a very lovely goldfish bowl, but still it was a shock the first time someone walked in without knocking and started to look around. It apparently never occurred to this gentleman, who had lived in the headmaster's house when he was a student some fifty years back, that the place might no longer be the quasi-dormitory that it was in the days of that bachelor headmaster.

The sociologist David Riesman coined a phrase to describe the type of official residence in which we lived: an old-style university mausoleum. I could go on at length about our mausoleum experience, and I will tell more stories in the course of this book, but for now I have said enough to make my point. We had no idea what life was going to be like in that home; we blithely moved in, confident that we could live there happily. Perhaps if we had not been so swept away by the glamour of it, we would have noted a few of the things that were going to make us uncomfortable and put some issues on the table. We had few reservations and expressed none of them, and it was only as events unfolded that we began to comprehend how trying it was going to be to live in this place.

Another way in which those big, old mansions harbor unpleasant surprises relates to their upkeep. Playing steward to such real estate is a weighty responsibility, and repair calls can be a weekly experience. It seems so obvious to me now, that a house three times as large and three times as old as anything we had ever lived in was going to be a different animal altogether where maintenance was concerned; yet when we first looked at the official residence this thought did not cross our minds.

For each mansion which houses someone who is quite happy to oversee it I suspect there is another in which the residents would really rather be doing other things. Sometimes the occupants don't want to shoulder the caretaking responsibility but also don't want to lose privacy and control by turning the business over to a house manager. And that is why you occasionally find a grand old mansion that is sadly run-down inside. When I first encountered this phenomenon I couldn't understand how anyone could allow a beautiful home to deteriorate; now I do.

Our mausoleum experience lasted four years, and then we got lucky. The school head's house sat so close to the administration building that it was clearly an ideal location for offices, and as the pressure for more office space grew, more and more eyes were cast longingly at this hulking structure. Finally the pressure was great enough for the trustees to start hinting that we might need to move elsewhere. We could hardly mask our hope and joy as plans went forward for a new house in a better location on campus.

Why does the mausoleum type of residence persist? There are many reasons, and perhaps first among them is the not-inconsiderable weight of tradition. These magnificent homes *seem* like the proper way to house a hard-working college president or school head; and a handsome, stately official residence makes everyone proud. Look around one of these places and it is easy to imagine gracious sit-down dinners for twelve, or twenty, or thirty. You can picture the delicate crystal, the silver and the candelabra here, the elegant accoutrements which would look so out of place in any other spot on campus. Yes, this is the way it should be!

I was susceptible to that feeling myself, before I actually lived in an official residence. The reality bore little relation to the scenes I had pictured in my mind. The total number of guests invited to the residence over the course of a year must have run close to a thousand. At a typical indoor party the house was filled with people standing in groups. Only the first few guests could actually observe what the well-decorated rooms looked like below shoulder level; all the fine upholstered furniture was there not to be sat upon, but to be spilled upon. And delicate crystal? Forget it! We pulled out all the stops and hosted an elegant dinner party, with crystal, silver and the best china, perhaps once a year. With dozens of functions to host and hundreds of people to entertain, devoting so much labor to a small gathering seemed highly impractical.

When we first saw the official residence we, like the search committee and many people connected with the institution, considered it an attraction. And that is another reason that such places persist. To the uninitiated, they seem too good to be true. So much space, free of charge, cleaning help provided, redecorating budget available. What's not to like?

To my mind the only good reason for a mausoleum to persist is that it provides a very special venue for the leader's entertaining. The cultivation of constituents is a sizeable and important duty of today's school heads and college and university presidents. And yet, I think a tastefully-decorated room on campus, strictly reserved for the leader's entertaining, might serve just as well—and perhaps better. A place which was designed to provide flexibility for groups of different sizes, accessibility for the handicapped, and coatroom and restroom facilities sufficient for the largest parties would beat out any mausoleum I have known. And the host and hostess could simply go home when they were ready for the party to end! If the bulk of official entertaining happened not at the residence but elsewhere on campus, events at the residence would recover the cachet they once had.

The mausoleum-type residence is slowly giving way. In some places it is still used for entertaining, but the leader doesn't actually live there. Or the leader might make it the primary residence but, for sanity's sake, keep a getaway on the side. Occasionally I hear that an institution plans to expand rather than shrink the official residence. There may well be good reasons to do that, but I wonder whether such changes sometimes come about because of a notion that a huge residence in the traditional style is a sign that an institution has arrived. It might rather be the mark of an institution that has been standing still.

The idea of offering a residence that relieves the leader of all housing worries is at base well-intentioned. But such housing would be the antithesis of the old-style university mausoleum. It would not be a place that was expected to both house the family and host armies of guests, two fundamentally different purposes that seldom share the same premises with any grace. It would be an easily-managed place, a place of peace and quiet and privacy in a residential neighborhood, a place that only a few very special guests would ever see.

In an era when the pressure on academic leaders has grown nigh to unbearable, when people are asking how these pressures can be eased, the housing question must be considered. If an official residence passes the "old-style university mausoleum" test, it is almost surely adding to the burden the leader is bearing. Housing him or her in a place that constitutes a drain on time and energy makes no sense. And I have not mentioned the heavy financial and environmental costs associated with such a place, both of which are harder to justify with each passing year. It is time, I think, to blow away the vapors that envelope official residences of the traditional type, time to weigh what they offer against what they cost.

Searching for the Cracks. If you are going to live in an official residence, it may be bigger, more elegant, better equipped and more fully staffed than any place you ever dreamed of living in. Large residences can be fine places to live if the spaces have been designed with the modern family in mind. They tend to carry with them the assumption that the leader will entertain large groups, but all the space makes this relatively easy, especially if someone has carefully thought it out, right through the coat-and-powder-room problems. However, if the residence is ideal for entertaining large groups, it might be hard for a small family to feel comfortable there. If it is comfortable for a family, it might be hard to entertain large groups. I believe that one has to be prepared to live with a few compromises; this housing is usually provided free of charge, after all. But the institution, in turn, should be prepared to spend some funds to make the house suit the new family's needs. If there is no budget to do this, no assurances that it will be done, I would be concerned.

Take a good, hard-eyed look at the residence and imagine your family living there. Try to mentally transfer your daily routines into this house, to see the family moving about it through the whole of the day. You may be expecting to host a new type of houseguest, someone who is more official guest than friend. A separate guest wing is ideal, but not always a possibility. As you decide which room, or rooms, to designate for guests, it's good to consider how much those guests will be mixing in with the family. A dressing room separate from the master bedroom may sound like a great luxury. However, when your partner has a dense travel schedule the suitcase is always out, and a luggage rack becomes part of the standard furnishings. It is unpleasant, for several reasons, to have these things always in full sight in your bedroom. You might like having the family room right next to the kitchen, the way so many homes are designed these days. But if you are going to be doing a lot of entertaining at the residence, you may well find yourself with an occupying force of caterers in the kitchen on numerous occasions. Picture those long evenings when the guests have finally departed but the clean-up crew is just getting started. Will you be able to sit down and relax in the family room, if people are noisily washing up in the kitchen just a few feet away? Perhaps, in addition to that family room you will also need a small den, a more separate space, where you can escape on such occasions.

A spouse who is going to be actively involved needs space to accommodate files, calendars, a telephone and a computer to connect with the campus network. This should be a place where confidential material can be left lying around. Even in large residences, however, one eventually bumps up against the ceiling of available space. Carving out a niche in a guest bedroom is not a great solution, but it is one with which I have lived. In one residence my space was in the library, a somewhat public room where guests left their coats if it was cold or rainy, and through which they walked if we were entertaining in the back garden. I positioned my desk in a back corner of the room, facing inward so that I would notice anyone coming in either door. There was no room for a filing cabinet, so I kept any "sensitive" material face-down on the window bench behind my chair. I suspect that this arrangement was sufficient to keep visitors from prying into my business, but I will never really know.

A large house with sizeable grounds should come with the offer of cleaning and gardening help, should you want it. If these services are not offered, it may be because your predecessor preferred to handle it differently. That may be a clue; I would ask a lot of questions to find out why the previous administration handled things the way it did.

Sometimes more extensive household support is on offer—someone to cook family meals, help with childcare or do the laundry. We have never had, nor wished for, that much help, but it could make a significant difference for a spouse who wants to maintain a separate career. I think it is fair for the institution to foot a part of the expense, because important as these matters are, the leader-partner has little time to do his or her fair share of the chores.

No matter how you plan to live in an official residence, it is good to learn what preconceptions others have of the place. Is it seen primarily as a home, or as a venue for entertaining? That is to say, will groups expect to have the more public rooms at their disposal, whether or not the leader is to be part of the function in question?

You may be scratching your head at this point. A party in our home, to which we are not invited? Such expectations do exist at some institutions. Sometimes it comes about because a single person was rattling around, living in a huge official residence, and decided it would make good sense to let groups use the house for meetings and events. I don't think there's any reason new residents should be expected to make the house available in precisely the way their predecessors did. But should you decide you will allow such uses, you might want to consider how you would feed the family (or yourself) when some committee is using the kitchen and dining area, and the house is not fully available to you.

Often a residence which is used heavily for entertaining will be furnished at the institution's expense, at least with regard to those rooms which will have the most traffic. It can be hard to hide away your gorgeous Persian rug or the heirloom china, but think carefully before you decide to subject your favorite things to the wear and tear of official entertaining. At large parties elbows are bumped and food and drink go flying. Catering crews might not be aware of the value or delicacy of crystal or china. Will you be able to shrug it off when accidents happen to things you prize?

If the residence is more magnificent than any house you've ever lived in, you'll probably feel guilty asking for changes. You might spot some problem areas right away, but because you don't want to appear demanding or ungrateful, you are prepared to move in anyway and hope for the best. This is a mistake. Once your partner is thoroughly embroiled in the new job and is starting to identify what the institution as a whole needs, personal needs are likely to drop further and further down a growing list.

Everyone wants the new leader to get off to a good start. Most institutions expect that there will be one-time expenses during the transition period, and they may have reserved funds for the purpose. This is the time to make your wishes known. If the funds are not enough to cover the changes you feel you need, at least you will have called attention to the problems. A poor home situation, especially if there is little hope for correction, is a slow poison.

I would emphasize here that I am talking about *needs* and not *tastes*. A residence that is well-decorated, but to someone else's taste and not your own, can present a touchy problem. The board may be quite willing to foot the bill for redecoration, but this is an area where the difference between the lifestyle of a typical board member, and that of most members of the other constituencies, may come into play. Redecorating that is perceived as unnecessary, done just because it satisfies someone's personal whim, is an easy way for new residents to get off on the wrong foot.

I am someone who cares a great deal about my personal surroundings. I've been very fortunate that the residences that I've wanted to change more to my liking have been due for some redecorating. The institutions have footed the bill for the most part. But whenever I feel I really want to change something for my own pleasure, and not because it needs replacing or updating, I will go ahead—and pay for it myself.

It probably goes without saying that if there are projects on the planning boards, renovations that were being considered by the previous administration, it is wise to put major changes on hold. Any plans that were made to suit your predecessors' personal needs and uses of the residence may, or may not, suit you and your family. It can be disappointing news for the gardener, who is beginning to see his or her dream come to fruition, or for the caterer, who has been struggling with inadequate kitchen facilities. But you can't be sure at this early stage how you will respond to life in the residence. By the same token, it may not be wise to rush in with requests for major changes you think you need. The more money that is spent altering the residence to please you, the harder it will be to negotiate your way out of it, should it prove unlivable.

The Male Point of View: "If a prospective spouse called me today I would say that if it feels glamorous they are doing something wrong."

3

On Getting Information and Giving Intelligent Support

Information Is the Key. To my mind it's a toss-up whether the greatest nuisance for a spouse is not having enough information, or having it wrong. Whether a spouse is actively involved in institutional affairs or a quiet supporter behind the scenes, good spousework hinges on information. Knowledge and understanding make it possible for us to support our partners intelligently, make it possible for us to interact with others with tact and grace. People tend to assume that spouses know everything, yet we may again and again be caught out of the loop. True, I have easy access to the person who *does* know virtually everything. But even if it were possible for my husband to keep me clued in on every new development, it is not the way I would want to spend my time with him.

In my many years of spousework I have often felt like I was trying to understand an important message from a radio broadcast that was full of static. There can be a lot of frustration, sometimes arising from the spouse's unique situation. At one institution I was given a computer, an e-mail account and access to the college network, and I thought I was set to receive the information that would be general knowledge on campus. Then I began to notice a problem. My husband would mention an announcement that had been distributed over the network, and I would have no idea what he was talking about. For some reason I was not receiving these mass broadcasts. I had to nag a while before the information technology office provided an explanation. Because I was neither enrolled as a student nor on the payroll, I had no place on any of the distribution lists. More time passed before they addressed the problem and figured out a way to correct it.

A spouse who is unfamiliar with the campus can easily feel overwhelmed. There is so much going on, so many players, and so much history that has gone before, some of it still highly relevant. New information courses through the campus all day, every day. On the mundane level each campus has its own procedures and access routes, whether it's a matter of checking out library books or getting tickets for an event. At very small institutions there may be a "one big family" atmosphere accompanied by the assumption that everyone knows, as soon as they happen, about engagements, births and illnesses, and even about the deaths of elderly parents that sometimes call community members away.

Clearly, information must come from a number of different sources. I believe it behooves the spouse to wade in and go after the information, rather than expecting the leader to relay all that needs to be known. The couple has to be in constant communication, of course, but when you *can* spend time together, why fritter it away talking about the nuts and bolts of campus life that just about any-one could explain to you?

Getting Information from Everyone but Your Partner. When we have transferred to a new campus, I've found that a few hours spent studying the cam-pus viewbook, the publication that is given to prospective students, is invaluable. In fact, it's a good idea to keep the latest edition handy. You might be brand-new to the institution, but you will constantly be faced with questions from those who know even less than you do: the parents of new or prospective students, visiting lecturers, and so forth. These folks may be unaware that you are practically a stranger yourself, and so they will ask you almost anything.

My passion for local history has served me well. I started reading any available written histories of several of the institutions we've served, even before we moved to campus. I was simply curious, but what I found was that this reading material supplied me with a lot of small talk, a way to demonstrate my interest in the insti-tution, and a leg up on understanding what engines were pushing events on cam-pus.

Special-purpose publications appear from time to time, at the kick-off of a fund-raising campaign, for example. It does not always occur to those who see this material through the publication process that I might like to have copies, indeed that I might need them. I am always on the look-out for new brochures and publications I haven't seen before.

As for more ephemeral matters, I've learned how to get the information I need quickly and efficiently, and how to avoid being overloaded with a lot of facts I don't really want. I get on the distribution list for the daily and weekly campus publications which are of interest; I may not be up-to-date in reading them, but at least I have them near at hand. I have a standing order with my contacts in the alumni, development, and parent-relations offices, the people who co-ordinate events that my husband and I host. They know that I like to have the guest list a week ahead of time, together with brief notations if there's anything in particular I should know about someone. (This is how you are forewarned about the guy whose family donated the portrait that used to hang over the mantle in the living room!) We have a facsimile machine at the residence, and campus mail is delivered to our door. I receive a lot of information via e-mail, but those who are my frequent contacts know I do not want to be held hostage by my computer. I check my e-mail for messages once a day. I do it more often than that only when it is convenient.

Through my keyboard I can access my partner's electronic calendar. I can find out where he is, or will be, and get a general idea of what's up. That saves a lot of phone calls to his office staff. When my husband travels, his staff sends me a copy of his itinerary that includes telephone numbers for the hotels he'll stay in. I have figured out pretty well how to keep up with his comings and goings, but keeping up with everything else on campus is a daily challenge. How many times have I thought I knew what to expect on a particular day, only to find out that I had an early draft of the plan and never received the final update? It still happens, more often than I like to admit. Most often it happens when those major week-ends, like commencement and reunion, come around. Since I like to have some input into the planning of events for which we will be named as hosts, I meet with the appropriate staff members, and those meetings may take place many months before the event. I might take away the first draft of the schedule and carefully file it. Such things are usually marked "Draft", and I've found it's a good idea to highlight that word with a marker before I file the papers. I have learned to put non-specific reminders on my calendar when the date is still months off—"reception PM" instead of "reception 5:30–7 PM". A week or two before the actual event I make sure that I have the up-to-the-minute details.

Using Information Wisely. The alumni, development and parent-relations offices all have mounds of data on the folks in their respective constituencies. In the early days, when I asked for some information about the people we would be entertaining, I got much, much more than I wanted. I was looking for something that might point to a topic of conversation with a total stranger, and I didn't think very much about the best way to make use of the information I had gleaned. At some point I began to notice that, once in a while, a guest seemed to be surprised, even discomfited, by how much I knew about him or her. I started to see a pattern in these instances, and that led me to analyze the kinds of information I was receiving. Basically, it was the same data that my husband was getting. Part of it was current, fairly public information: that someone is a member of the family that endowed a chair; that she is a former trustee or the winner of some alumni prize; that he is the tenth member of his family to attend the institution. Part of it was confidential, the giving history/possible cultivation information. And part of it was in the public realm but not so current, such as data going back to the student days of alumni. An item in this third category can be very useful, but I was not being at all cagey about using this type of information. If I noted a detail that seemed to be promising fodder for conversation, I might introduce it in a rather abrupt way: "I think you grew up in Alaska. What was that like?" No wonder that I startled some people, as I dragged up information from distant pasts. If I knew that much, what else did I know? When I looked at the situation from a guest's point of view I could see that I needed to modify my approach. These days I would say something like, "I see [from your nametag] that you live in Idaho. Are you from that region originally?"—hoping to solicit from my guest that which I already knew, that he/she actually grew up in Alaska.

This was one of the ways in which I lagged behind my husband. It is part of his job to know how best to use a specific item of information; it comes with thinking politically. My husband was accustomed to thinking that way, but I wasn't. In fact, I used to feel that political thinking was tantamount to sneaky behavior, and I wanted no part of it. Now I know that I must think politically if I want to do a decent job as the spouse.

After pondering my conversational habits I became more specific about requesting information about the people I was to meet. What is most desirable and important for me to know is information in the first category, that which is currently in the realm of public knowledge but which I, being a newcomer, may not know. The other two categories might be useful if I'm expecting to spend hours or days with a particular person, but that does not happen as often. And now that I can better define what information I want before a party, I don't have to discard so much confidential data, which can be a nuisance since one really should go to the trouble of shredding the paper.

Intelligent Support: From Information to Understanding. I indicated in the first chapter that I was a slow learner when it came to playing my role as supportive spouse. I didn't realize that being a sympathetic listener was only the starting point. But I was at a disadvantage even there, one that was imposed upon us by circumstances. When we started out in our first official residence, we fell into a pre-dinner routine on those evenings when my husband had an hour or two to relax at home. We would sit and talk for a while in the family room; he would give me a quick recap of the day's events, and I imagined that I was staying pretty well-informed. After twenty or thirty minutes I would leave him alone to read the mail and the newspaper while I went downstairs to the kitchen to prepare supper. This was not an ideal arrangement; we preferred the layout of our old home, where the kitchen opened onto the family room and we weren't so separated during these hours. In those days we would both move back and forth from kitchen to family room and swap bits of news from the day as they popped into our heads. But now we were living in this grand house, where the inconvenient placement of the family room just seemed like one of the trade-offs for all the luxuries. I tried to make a virtue of it, thinking that my husband was looking forward to turning his attention to something other than campus matters. The sooner I let him concentrate on his newspaper, the better.

After a few years I was well-acquainted with campus life and the major players associated with the institution. I thought I was staying informed, and certainly I was privy to all kinds of confidential information. But nonetheless I was at that point still skimming along the surface of an information ocean. I could spell out what the big issues were, but I had only a very superficial understanding of them. I hadn't yet broken through to the good stuff, to the best, most interesting kind of spousework, partly because of my own hesitation to pester my husband with questions.

I had become involved with the school in my own way, doing research for an alumnus who was writing the history of the institution. I enjoyed this work immensely, and it was helping to restore a sense of identity—a personal identity, as distinguished from a marital identity. Delving into the old files gave me a new perspective on the institution. And it was a boon for my husband, since I shared with him the charming anecdotes and intriguing facts I discovered in the course of my work, and he often used them in his speeches. I was starting to think that this state of affairs was probably as good as it was going to get, that my vague hopes for some more intense form of sharing had been unrealistic.

In fact, I was getting very close to what I had been looking for. I may have had a sense that something was still missing, but I didn't know what it was or how to get it. Then, quite serendipitously, I blundered into it.

During our fourth year the trustees decided to build a new house for the school head, and we had the pleasure of contributing to the design. We knew we wanted a sitting area adjoining the kitchen, so that we could be together while dinner preparations were underway. Once we moved into that new house we happily fell back into the old routine that we had enjoyed in our former life, being close to each other as dinner was being prepared, exchanging information in a more relaxed and thoughtful way. There was no sense of running down a checklist of items we needed to share with each other and then declaring the meeting over. Our discussions became more leisurely, and as I began the cooking I would continue thinking about what I had learned and would ask questions or pass along new thoughts as they occurred to me. My understanding of campus affairs began to deepen, and I became a better sounding board for my husband's ideas. I could offer suggestions and insights that were worth his consideration. I might suggest a pertinent and timely topic, when he needed to write a column for some publication, or a different way of framing the material when he was working on a speech. These kinds of contributions remained, of course, very much behind the scenes. But I really didn't care that much. I was playing a more significant role, and that was richly satisfying. I had always been a team member, for sure, but mostly a bench-warmer. Now I was in the game.

Though I believe that my personality is less than ideal for a person in my position, there is one trait that serves me very well. I am a keen student of human behavior. I can happily spend hours analyzing a person's actions, trying to understand what motivated him or her to behave in a particular way. An academic leader's career is thoroughly people-oriented; it provides endless material for contemplation along these lines. It may be in this area that I am most useful as a sounding board for my husband's thoughts.

I have asked myself whether I could have sped up the process of learning to give support in an intelligent way. The simple realization that I had much to learn, that I wasn't fully armed with the support skills I was going to need, would surely have helped. But I think I also could have looked to my husband to be not only a source of information but a teacher. I could have asked more advice when we were starting out. For example, when a constituent asked me a question that left me fumbling for an answer, I could have consulted with my husband afterward and asked him how he would have responded. I recall an instance when the parent of a newly-enrolled student tried to pin me down by asking me, "What are the best departments on campus?" I knew which departments were generally touted as the best, but I didn't want to open myself to accusations of partiality. I wriggled out of giving the direct answer this parent surely wanted but was not entirely happy with my response. If I had reported that experience to my husband and asked for his advice, I would have come away with some insight into how he manages tricky questions, insight into the skills he had already developed and I had yet to master.

It cheers me to remember that, in one way, I was giving intelligent support right from the start, without even trying. I refer to a kind of support which comes not so much from information as from shared experience. No matter what spouses have been led to expect, they soon find that there is no zero on the scale of involvement. Spouses share with the leaders the strain of being "living logos" (a phrase coined by the sociologist David Riesman). Living logos represent the institutions they are connected with, always and everywhere. They learn to temper their personal opinions accordingly. This means that on a day-to-day basis, with almost everyone they meet, both leaders and spouses have their guards up; they are on their best behavior. On a day-to-day basis it may be only in each other's company that they can revert to their authentic selves. It may be only in each other's company that either of them can vent any pent-up feelings.

This constraint is, on its flip side, a gift to the couple, a natural bond. I didn't apprehend this at the start, when the very idea that either one of us might have negative feelings was a little bit scary. But from the beginning those moments when we could let down together at the end of the day seemed special. Only much later did I grasp that you can support someone in a positive way by just granting them a little time to be negative.

Intelligent Support vs. the "Power behind the Throne". A spouse who knows the academy backwards and forwards, from experience as a faculty member or an administrator, has a head-start in becoming a source of intelligent support. But I have learned from other spouses that this is not altogether an enviable position. That is because people may be rather too quick in assuming that the spouse is providing a great deal of advice and has huge influence over the new leader. Unfortunately, gender can be part of the issue when, for example, an institution has a woman at its head for the first time. But experience alone can set up the same scenario.

It is an awkward situation when a spouse realizes that some constituents are assuming too much spousal influence. It can also be a painful situation for a spouse who takes great pride in his or her partner's achievements. Most of us spouses are happy to receive a little credit for our contributions, and at first glance there seems to be no harm in occasionally letting folks give us more credit than is actually due. But misperceptions in this area can lead to trouble. I'm of the opinion that even when a spouse is aware that he or she has made a brilliant contribution, any public acknowledgment should come directly from the academic leader—not from the spouse, and not from any others who believe they know the source of the inspiration. Complete self-effacement, or denial of any contribution at all, may be too much to expect of any mortal, and especially of a spouse who is feeling ego-bruised (as many of us do in the beginning). So I tell myself that an air of mystery is attractive. Who doesn't want to feel attractive?

Being Discreet and a Keeper of Secrets. Implicit in all this is the expectation that the spouse is a solid, trustworthy keeper of secrets and is always careful to be discreet. Naturally we will have our own opinions about, and reactions to, people we encounter. Most of the time it is wise to keep to ourselves negative opinions about people connected with the institution—anyone in any constituency, no matter how obvious it is that the person in question has acted like a complete jerk, or has been mean and nasty to us or our partners. Being discreet to such an extent is difficult, and for those of us who are used to speaking out freely, learning to hold back can be quite a challenge. But it is good practice for those times when keeping discreet is most painful and most necessary.

You can probably imagine what I mean when I refer to "those times". When your partner is under attack for some unpopular decision, and *you* know that the attackers would not be so critical if only they knew the full story, quite naturally you want to stand up and show whose side you are on, maybe even drop a hint that it is the only side that anyone "in the know" could possibly be on.

These occasions are awful for those of us who partner academic leaders. To my mind it is the most painful part of spousework—not being able to openly defend one's mate. It may be especially hard for the males among us. When a female leader is under attack, a male spouse who is protective of his wife might find himself tempted to throw a punch. Whether the punch is verbal or physical, it goes without saying that that is a path no one should go down.

When someone alludes in conversation to some trouble on campus, the best response I've come up with is, "It is a very painful situation for everybody." And if they persist in prying (or trying to support me, which may come to the same thing), I sigh and say, "It is very painful for everyone involved, as I said. Let's change the subject."

Some presidents and school heads may believe that it is best to protect their spouses, to shield them from the knowledge of acute problems. I personally don't think this is a good idea, unless the spouse is likely to be unable to keep a confidence, or is so burdened by other problems that one more would constitute an overload. For one thing, how can a spouse ever hope to give intelligent support if intelligence is being withheld? For another thing, spouses can sense trouble, and if they have no explanation of what the problem is, they can imagine almost anything. Finally, if the leader is being attacked, either in print or in conversations on campus, I believe it is healthy for the spouse to know the facts so that he or she can feel secure in the belief that the leader's decision was well-advised. A spouse who knows the true state of affairs can also offer reassurance to the couple's children, for often they, too, can sense when something has gone wrong.

But perhaps I am only looking for further justification for my own need to know. I am a born worrier whose antennae are always up. When trouble is afoot I am better off knowing what's the matter than imagining my own scenarios. I don't need a lot of detail. Other spouses may not want to be privy to certain kinds of confidential information, when, for example, someone is about to lose a job. They want to avoid an awkward situation, should they encounter that person socially. I think each of us needs to consider what we want to know, what we need to know, and how much information we are willing to harbor and protect.

Being discreet, of course, involves more than keeping the big cats in their bags. With hordes of information come little cats as well. If it is hard to keep up with what is happening on campus, it is even harder to keep track of who knows what at any point in time. To stop myself from inadvertently divulging semi-secrets, I assume that just about everything I hear from my partner is confidential. When I see it in print, or hear it on the street, then I can let down my guard.

Oftentimes a change that is under consideration seems utterly inconsequential to me, in terms of its effect on the community. But I have learned that, nearly always, *someone* has a vested interest in the matter. A particular program that is being re-evaluated was someone's pet project. Or someone's job description might have to change, and perhaps that will mean a loss of working hours or of prestige. I don't want to have to think each matter through, examining it for its potential impact on everyone in the community. It's easier, and safer, for me to simply assume that every matter is a sensitive one.

Even information that is generally known on campus, but not officially announced, is best left alone. In one of our first years a newspaper reporter called our house and asked if I could confirm that a certain student had been dismissed. I was usually aware of the problem when a student was in trouble, because deans, teachers and parents suddenly started calling the house to talk to my husband. In this particular case, I knew that the student had been expelled a few days before; it was no big secret. But here was someone calling long distance to ask for confirmation, and furthermore, he had identified himself as a reporter. It just didn't smell right to me. And sure enough, I later learned what was behind the call. The student had a parent in a high-profile elected position, and the opposition was looking for dirt. No one ever told me, "Don't talk to reporters"—but after this experience I decided it would be a fine rule to impose upon myself.

Lastly, there is the matter of handling with discretion information about oneself. I have come to dread inquiries from students who want to interview me. My feelings about my position are complicated, and I don't believe anyone could understand the nuances on the basis of a brief interview. When I am interviewed I ask to see the article before it goes to press so that I can correct facts and misperceptions. Rare is the student reporter who allows enough time for this, and even rarer is the one who actually manages to get the corrections into print. It seems that some breakdown along the way is inevitable. Next time I will do as my husband suggests, requiring the student to bring along a tape recorder. And I am prepared to be hard-nosed if he or she forgets!

At one and the same time, I know too much and I know too little. I think I keep up-to-date about what's going on, but occasionally I have an odd encounter and wonder whether people are pumping me for information I simply don't have. The eyebrow is raised, the voice is dropped, and I get the definite feeling that my interlocutor is sending me a message—but I have no notion what it is. So I say "Ummm" or bow my head to show that I got the message, if there *was* one. Later I'll ask my husband if something is happening that this person might know about. Sometimes our two heads together can't figure it out, and we drop the incident into our bag of funny little secrets. It's really rather delicious.

The Male Point of View: "I had to give up trying to be her knight in shining armor. It is difficult, when my wife offloads her day, just to keep my mouth shut and listen. I have learned to listen more than offer solutions, since she is not seeking help but just dumping the crud out."

4

Life in an Official Residence

The Public Life at Home. For most people home is a refuge, a private world we construct for our own comfort. I could list beforehand all sorts of ways in which living in an official residence was going to be different from living in a home of our own, but there was a truckload of differences I could never have imagined. We expected that we would lose a lot of privacy and have less control of our home life in a few obvious ways. All this required some major adjustments, not only to the outward changes but also to the subtle, unforeseen pressures that accompanied them. While I anticipated that loss of privacy would be a major issue for me, I was somewhat surprised to find that loss of control was at least as challenging. I was used to choosing the people who would clean my house, mow my lawn, repair my leaking pipes, used to deciding whether to repair or replace an appliance, whether to put paint or wallpaper on the walls. I have found it hard to cede that kind of control to others.

I know that I risk sounding spoiled and ungrateful, but I will wade in because this has been a significant problem for me and may be for others as well. Ceding so much responsibility for our home life makes me feel infantilized. I am not sure it's healthy. Grown-ups want, and perhaps need, to take care of themselves. I regularly remind myself how fortunate we are, not to have to worry about so many details, and yet I chafe. I would love to just sit back and enjoy it, but there is something in me that prevents that from happening.

When people ask me what it is like, living in a beautiful old house imbedded on a college campus, I sometimes answer that it is like living on a film set. I am accustomed to this life, and yet it doesn't feel quite real. I don't quite believe it. For example, being at home, behind locked doors, would—or so you would think—insure a feeling of privacy. But it doesn't. Everybody knows where we live, and keys to the residence are in the hands of a number of different people. There's a sense that we are sitting ducks and need to be watchful, even expectant. This feeling rises and falls for my husband and me with the number of students on campus, but even when the term ends and the students go home it isn't easy to shake it.

The most startling thing that ever happened to us in the years of occupying different residences was an incident that interrupted our sleep one night. In the end it was comical, though it might not have seemed so if I had not been well-seasoned by life in this type of domicile. On this particular night we were asleep in the bedroom; the door was closed, to keep out the bats who had taken up residence with us. I woke up suddenly and saw a light through the gap under the door; it seemed to be sweeping left and right out in the hallway. I wasn't aware of hearing any sound, but I must have somehow had an inkling what was happening, because I wasn't afraid. I shook my husband's shoulder and said, "Somebody is in the house." He was too groggy for the message to get through to him, so I got up, went over to the door and opened it a few inches. I could see a dark mass moving down the hall, the beam of a flashlight swinging ahead of it. I said, in a voice that no doubt sounded very loud in the still of the night, "That had better be Security out there." And so it was; the poor security officer almost had a heart attack.

We had not set our security alarm that night, but for reasons of its own it had gone off. That is to say, it sounded in the Office of Security and Safety, but not inside the house. Two security officers came over to check the residence, and seeing that there were no lights turned on inside they naturally assumed we were out of town. So they unlocked the door and came in to take a look around.

You will probably never, ever have an incident like this. I relate the story because of what it conveys about life in an official residence. I didn't panic when I was awakened that night, and that was pretty remarkable. I think I stayed calm because I exist—waking or sleeping—in a constant state of expectation that, at any moment, there could be an intrusion on my privacy. I felt quite sure that the residence was not being burgled, though had this happened in our own home I would have been equally sure that it *was* a burglar. This ever-present sense of expectation that goes with living in a residence can in itself be tiring; it's the main reason we maintain a home of our own to which we can retreat. It is the only place where we can truly, truly relax and refresh ourselves.

Living in residences has changed my attitude toward windows. I used to think of them as places for me to look *out,* whereas now I think of them as places for others to look *in.* If I were living in an ordinary house in an ordinary neighborhood, I might enjoy having a window over the kitchen sink which looked out onto the front walk. However, if I were in the business of designing official residences, I would always position that window to look over a secluded garden.

It was disconcerting to us to realize how interested people are in an official residence and its occupants. On the boarding school campus, while we were sitting quietly at home in the evening, some of the students passing by were noting the pattern of lights that were turned on. We know this because once in a while students were guileless enough to actually tell us that they had figured out which room was the master bedroom. Now, living just on the edge of a college campus, we have fewer students walking by and more townspeople. When I stand at a window and look out, I notice that many passersby look intently at the residence; sometimes they see me in the window and wave cheerily, even if they are perfect strangers.

This kind of thing was extremely annoying to me when I was still unseasoned. I sometimes felt like crying, "Geez, aren't we on display enough without people positively staring into our windows?" I'm still a very private person, but I have made peace with some behaviors I used to consider invasions of privacy. If you've ever been to England, perhaps you have gone to Buckingham Palace and stood outside for a while. You may have set out to see the changing of the guards, or to observe the beauty of the place, but I wonder how many of us are also hoping that we might just catch a glimpse of something else—someone coming or going who might give us a clue about the lives of the people inside. There's a mystique about a place like Buckingham Palace.

Well, forgive me for this grandiose comparison, but I think the same sort of mystique attaches itself to a president's or school head's residence. You have to admit that our lives in these places seem glamorous. Flowers are delivered, caterers come and go, the grounds are kept in topnotch condition. At any moment that famous alum who is visiting campus might step out the front door. This is a life set apart, and naturally some of those who pass by find it fascinating. Such interest is rather benign; there's nothing malicious about it. I save my exasperation for those who find the residence the obvious target for childish pranks.

If those who pass by your home seem to be more interested in you than you are used to, those who come into the house to perform some task may be as well. Most of the maintenance, repairs and renovations that our various residences have required were handled by institutional staff. The institution is likely to keep members of all the skilled-trades groups on staff, full-time and, in some cases, on call around the clock.

Any time you call for a staff member to make repairs at the residence, it is not simply a work-order. There is an added social aspect, since you are all connected with the same institution. It is quite different from the interactions you used to have with, say, the plumber who fixed the pipes in your private home. In that case, you did not expect to have a social relationship develop between you; in fact, you probably hoped that you wouldn't see the plumber again for a good, long time, because when you did, it was likely to mean another plumbing bill. You could virtually ignore this person without seeming arrogant or rude. At the official residence, you may be chafing to get back to your own work while repair people complete theirs, but campus personnel are likely to have no notion of that. They understand that the leader is a busy person, but they may see the spouse as someone who is just hanging around. In fact, for all they know that may be what the spouse does all day, every day.

The added social aspect in an official residence can seem invasive, and it means added time. However, it has its own importance. I have been guilty in the past of being impatient with this, especially during one super-busy week when we were getting ready for one of our first parties in a new residence. The house was going through a period of ill health, and we had called in a carpenter, an electrician, a phone-repair person, a plumber and some painters—five discrete issues that had to be attended to. We figured that the only skilled trade we had left out was HVAC. (That's the acronym for the heating, ventilation and air-conditioning folk—something I never needed to know when my husband was a college professor.) We were lucky to get all the repairs done. One of the advantages of living in an official residence is that the institution's repair and maintenance crews give us priority. They are frequently willing to drop everything and come right away.

The reason that week sticks in my memory is that the repair calls, with their attendant getting-to-know-you sessions, ate up a lot of my time and much of my social energy. I started each morning with a mental list of what I wanted to accomplish that day, and the residence threw these obstacles in my course. By the time the guests started arriving on Friday evening I was thoroughly frustrated, and my appetite for meeting new people was gone.

Now, when there is a run of repair work like that, or when a particular repair is going to take a couple of days, I might suggest that we do a patch job and postpone the more time-consuming, thorough repair work until a date when the family is out of town. The security squad can let repair people in during our absence. This is a service to which the typical homeowner does not have access, and we make the most of it.

Differing Needs for Privacy. The human need for privacy is one of the things that distinguish us from other animals. But just how much each one of us needs can vary from person to person. My husband and I had been married for over twenty years when we moved into our first official residence, and we thought we knew each other pretty well. So we were surprised to discover an area where we knew very little about each other—our individual needs for privacy.

We were both adjusting to the reduction of privacy in our lives, and I think we assumed that the amount of adjustment was about the same for each. Then one day something happened that made it clear that I was feeling more uncomfortable, more "invaded", than my husband was. I was at home that day when he came in with a family that was looking around campus. As I recall, it was the family of a prospective applicant. I happened to be on the ground floor when the group came in, so I bumped into them—or rather, they bumped into me. The visitors had a good look around that floor and then were escorted out.

My husband and I had agreed that the upper floors were to be kept private, that guests were not to be invited upstairs unless they were staying overnight. But we had never discussed impromptu house tours. I made a mental note to myself: "He needs to call me before he walks in with someone, or at least he should duck his head in the door and let me know what's up before they all walk in. I'm going to talk to him about this tonight."

That evening I brought up the subject of the unexpected visitors. I fear I didn't stop with a simple regurgitation of the mental note I'd made. I remember saying something like, "This wasn't even a prospective student! They were only *thinking* about applying!" We were both tired, and I was irritated, and it wasn't the best time to discuss the issue. Or maybe it was—because we came to understand that this really *was* an issue for me, while it wasn't for him. I was happy to invite hundreds of people I didn't know to parties, and I would have been happy to give a pre-arranged tour to an important visitor or someone who had a really good reason for wanting to see the house. But I drew the line at unannounced house tours and what I perceived to be casual tourists, and my husband wasn't drawing the line in the same place. Once he understood how I felt, once we understood that our needs for privacy were different, the problem dissolved.

The Cost of Living. America may be a throw-away society, but the academic institutions with which we have been connected seem to be exceptions. There's a tendency to hold onto things as long as possible. There seems to be a widespread feeling that it's always better to repair than to replace. I have lived with appliances so old that I have prayed the repair people wouldn't be able to find the necessary parts. (The internet has, alas, made it easier than ever to locate parts for older appliances.) I suspect skilled-trades workers get a lot of satisfaction from fixing up some hulking old appliance and making it purr. And if they are paid to be around full-time anyway, perhaps the "repair rather than replace" attitude is cost-effective overall.

There's an art to calculating the point of diminishing returns, of course. And this is where I have a bone to pick. I know that the hours spent by any skilled-trades worker will be billed to the residence's account at the appropriate rate. It doesn't matter that much, because the residence account is just one of the pockets in the huge overcoat of campus expenses. But I don't think that the costs of operating the residence are tracked in the same way that they might be in, say, a dormitory. I've sometimes wondered whether anyone who *does* have to worry about budgets is aware of the number of repair calls at the residence. Is anyone looking for that point of diminishing returns? In addition, repair calls are invasive, and they are more invasive in a home than in an office, because a home is basically a personal space. So sometimes, when it looks like an appliance is in a downward spiral, I begin to push the idea that it's time to give it up and put an end to the doctoring visits.

For eighteen years we have lived in one official residence or another, and we have never had any idea what the total annual cost of running the place has been. No one has ever talked to us about the budget for its operation. I know we are privileged in this way, and that a leader of a public institution, or of an institution of any type whose finances are precarious, may not have such a privilege. I am relieved that our institution doesn't expect us to account for every dollar. On the other hand, this is a bit worrisome: the perception of runaway costs associated with the official residence has brought more than one administration to its end. I feel uneasy about this privilege. We want to be responsible about spending the institution's money, and if anyone thought we weren't being responsible, we would want to know about it as soon as possible.

I used to wonder what would happen if, for example, there was an undetected leak in a pipe that was driving up a utility bill at the residence. How bad would it have to get before someone got up the nerve to ask us if we could explain why a particular bill was so high? At one post a staff member actually did call to ask about a water bill that seemed to be running away. (He did not realize that the grounds crew had run a hose from our house so that they could give constant water to a large tree that had recently been transplanted.) Somehow that employee felt safe in doing this, probably because my husband was regularly sending out signals that his administration was budget-conscious. Still, I think it took a lot of nerve, and perhaps not everyone would risk it.

I admit that I'm a born worrier, but I know that my cohorts at other institutions are sometimes perplexed by this same matter. It pertains not only to running the residence but also to entertaining issues. Should we be serving caviar or potato chips? What's an appropriate amount to spend on the wine for a party? It's a tricky business, and I think you have to feel your way along this path, find out what you are comfortable with, and somehow ascertain what the institution is comfortable with. And that may vary from year to year, as the financial health of the institution waxes and wanes.

Keeping Your Sense of Humor. Sometimes you just have to laugh. Life in an official residence can never be entirely predictable. You may carefully choose the absolutely perfect color to paint the dining room and come home to find that the painting crew has used the glossiest paint they could find. But, of course! These are the same painters who work in the dormitories; they make those surfaces as glossy and easy to clean as they possibly can. There's no one to blame here; it's just a matter of two parties on different wave lengths, with neither one recognizing it ahead of time.

Being able to see the humor in things depends so much on keeping your perspective. When I was spending what seemed like way too much time on our first big redecorating project, I lost all sense of proportion. I was working with an interior designer for the first time in my life, and that alone was a learning experience: two perfectionists, previously unacquainted with each other, trying to come up with choices and solutions that pleased both of us. And then there were the trustees, the august personages who held the purse strings. I wanted to impress upon them that I had used the money wisely and well. I kept at it until I felt every swatch of fabric was right, was in fact *perfect*. Only after I began to relax did I remember that the residence was, after all, just a building, and its décor said little or nothing about me. That was about the same time I realized that on that day when all would be unveiled, the trustees were liable to be much more interested in the scotch on the rocks than the pillows on the sofa.

The Male Point of View: "One afternoon when [my wife] had come home early to change for an event, her assistant called her to say that she hadn't been able to calm down an angry student, and he was on his way over to talk to her. I went out in the yard and mucked around until the student arrived. When he showed up I intercepted him and asked if I could help him. He said, "I don't need any help from the *gardener*." That made me laugh, which was a good thing, because I was pretty angry myself and was ready to put hands on him."

5

Taking Ownership of Time

Standing Up for Yourself. For the most part this chapter is concerned with ways in which a spouse can help manage the time famine that is an ever-present fact of life for academic leaders. But many spouses have their own time-management issues. Perhaps they feel the leader's job threatens their ability to pursue their own careers. If they are not employed, perhaps they feel trapped when others want to lay claim to their time. If you can't honestly say you are just too busy, it's hard to say "no". I'm convinced, however, that it is important for a spouse to learn to say "no". With grace and tact, of course!

There is a story, probably apocryphal, about a spouse who secured a life-size cardboard image of herself to stand in for her. Many spouses, and academic leaders, can sympathize. There will always be occasions when so many people have to be moved through the reception line that a nod and a smile are the order of the day. It can feel like a waste of time. It might feel that way for the leader, too, but I don't know if any leader could avoid this entirely. Spouses, however, are vulnerable to being caught in other situations where their presence simply was not needed and their absence would not have been noticed. It happens when staff members reflexively include the spouse in each and every event, without thinking, and the spouse co-operates, without thinking. I put in my time at a couple of reunion dinners where I stood like a cardboard cut-out while my husband made a speech. I was not even introduced; I suspect the emcees of the dinner programs didn't know my name. Twice was enough. I no longer show up at those particular events. I feel that anyone who is getting caught, again and again, in situations like this is making him- or herself too available.

Awkwardness often arises when people make simple assumptions, expecting that the spouse will be available in the same ways that his or her predecessor was available. I think it is best to meet these situations head-on and name them for what they are. When expectations are being passed along, after the spouse has been assured that this would not happen, the best response is to fend it off—with a little finesse so no one feels they have blundered. I have a carefully-constructed reply: "I guess that's something my predecessor wished to do. I probably won't be involved in the same ways." If it's a task that must be assigned to someone I will add, "There must be somebody else who would enjoy doing that more than I would."

Of course, there may be occasions when there is no time to pass the task along to someone else, because the unacknowledged expectation surfaced too late. This happened to me in my first year as a headmaster's wife. Late in November our housekeeper informed me that in the past my predecessor had decorated the chapel for the annual Festival of Lessons and Carols. The school had a strong Christian tradition; the Festival was only a few days away, and it was a big deal. You can bet my heart skipped a beat. Is there anyone who has time to burn at that season of the year? I didn't see how I could ask someone else to do it, so I caved in and did it myself.

My mood brightened when it occurred to me that the simplest solution, candles and greens on the window sills, would also be the quickest and loveliest one. However, as we sat in the chapel on that fiercely cold evening, the congregation's attention was periodically drawn to the unscripted tinkling of breaking glass. Frigid air cascading down the windows was causing the hurricane glasses to shatter. Knowing that I was responsible for this, I could hardly breathe until the service was over. I believe that we all escaped unscathed. But, be warned! This is what comes of caving in to unwanted expectations.

Know that Every Minute is Precious. School heads and college presidents have heavy responsibilities and brutal schedules. It's the normal state of affairs when classes are in session. And yet very few people seem to have any appreciation of the fact that a leader's time is precious. The fact that leaders work at seeming unrushed, that they take the time for some idle chat with any constituent encountered by chance, probably fosters this lack of understanding among those whose contact with the head office is only occasional. That leaders appear so often in the audience at performances and in the grandstands at games, events that most people consider leisure-time activities, might contribute as well. The deeper mystery is why those who should have a thorough understanding of the issue—those who regularly schedule the leader's meetings, for example—often don't think in terms of making optimum use of the time available. When a lawyer or consultant, a doctor or dentist, bills his or her time in fifteen-minute increments, both those who assign the time slots on the schedule and those who consume them are aware of the value of that commodity. But on academic campuses, even though faculty and students feel chronically starved for time, we simply don't have this same mind-set. It must be due to some lingering idea that the academy is where we all sit back and reflect on things, where the leisurely pace fosters insight and inspiration. Hardly the case any more!

Even when he or she can see that a problem exists, a leader might be uncomfortable pointing out that time is being frittered away in an unproductive activity. It smacks of self-importance. And perhaps some staff member, or even one's predecessor, deemed the activity a worthy use of time. A good office manager will guard against the squandering of the leader's time, but it's a tricky enough business that I find there's plenty of room left for a spouse to step in once in a while. For example, it is just when the pace is most frantic that the leader needs to have time for what might seem, but is not at all, self-indulgent—the opportunity to exercise or otherwise engage in whatever one does as a stress buster. But *everybody* is so busy—how can he or she beg for an hour off for a run in the park? Sometimes the spouse is the perfect person to do the begging. I have been known to remind my husband's staff that we will all be happier if he has time to exercise.

My help seems most often to come in the form of the question, directed at my husband, "Is this really a good use of all that time?" It is perhaps easier for me to keep things in perspective in some ways. I am at a distance from those who assure my partner, "We should allow half a day for that meeting," or "This reception will take three hours". I am immune to those who win him over to such commitments, sometimes against his own better judgment. I see the time slot on the schedule and ask, "Does it really *need* to last that long?" With regard to repeated meetings on the same topic, I think it helps that I am not embroiled in the actual deliberations. Like fear, a sense of urgency can be infectious. But I am far enough away to avoid contamination, and this distance means I might assess the situation differently. Hearing my point of view helps my husband pull back for a moment and ponder whether an issue is getting blown out of proportion. With regard to travel, it helps that I like to have him home with me. I scan a jaded eye over his itinerary for an upcoming term and ask questions like, "Couldn't these two trips to the west coast be combined into one?" Often it's too late to change the plan, but I like to think that, after a while, my nagging and probing helps the people who design my husband's days to get the gist. Why not try—at least *try*—to keep a breather in the schedule for perhaps a half-hour each day? Sometimes a leisurely walk around the campus, breaking away and having a chance for a little reflection, is the single most valuable use of the leader's precious time. It is simply not wise, when an hour, or a day, unexpectedly opens up on the calendar, to always rush in to plug the hole as if some leadership opportunity were going to leak away.

What a blessing it is that the typical academic year includes a liberal sprinkling of vacations. The head office never shuts down completely during these times, but people seem to acknowledge the fact that it is wise for everyone to slow the pace and take a few hours off once in a while. Thoughts of spending time in favorite pursuits when the next break comes can help to keep the weary going. But a "feast or famine" diet is never healthy, and valued parts of one's psyche can wither.

When my husband became a headmaster, I found it ironic that he had trouble making time for the very sorts of activities that had made him such an attractive candidate in the first place. He is a thoughtful person who likes to read and to toss around ideas, who has a couple of hobbies about which he is passionate. I didn't want him to give up activities that meant so much to him, and I should think that the trustees who hired him wouldn't want that either. Part of my spousework involves encouraging my husband to keep in touch with passions like flyfishing, and trying to help him find the time to do so.

Rethinking the Chores. In our former lives we divided up the mundane chores. Now heavy travel schedules, and days which begin with breakfast appointments and end at 10 PM, won't accommodate rules for daily tasks like "He does the dishes, she takes out the garbage". Then there are those tasks which pop up now and then and can't be postponed for long. The college president has no time to take the car in to get a new inspection sticker; the headmaster can't spend an afternoon taking a sick dog to the vet. Or, if she or he does take time for such things it inevitably puts more pressure on the remaining hours of the week. I was willing to assume the tasks that my husband could no longer manage so easily, during the academic year at least. I made a conscious choice. Still, it was not simply a matter of my picking up what my partner had to drop. Even with my carefully-tended mindset, taking over chores that had traditionally been his caused me some aggravation. We came to refer to it as the changing-the-oil-in-the-car problem.

There was a time when my husband was committed, with quasi-religious fervor, to getting the oil changed in our cars every 3,000 miles. When he became a school head, I took over the oil-changing task, but I was not so fervent, and I had plenty of other things to keep me busy. When my husband fretted about the mounting miles, we had to sit down to try to reach a meeting of the minds. The discussion brought out a point that I think we already knew in our hearts but had not verbalized—that we simply could not expect to stay on top of things as we had before.

Of course, my husband was not seriously worried about compromising the integrity of our automobiles. Worry was in the air we breathed that first year. We remember the oil-change incident not because the stakes were so high, but because it was a clarifying moment. We no longer had time to indulge some of our old, comfortable and comforting habits. There have been many occasions since then when we called up that early memory, many other times when we've shaken our heads and said, "We just have to let that go now—it's like changing the oil in the car." But now we can smile at each other when we say it.

While we were able to let up on ourselves in some ways, I personally became more compulsive about some chores. Keeping the house neat and tidy and the cupboards well-stocked took on new importance—probably my way of responding to the loss of control of my life in other areas. With less time than before to run errands, I ran them more often. I hit the grocery store three times a week instead of once, because it was soothing to get it done, to check off something on my "to do" list. When it finally dawned on me that I was trading precious time for a fleeting sense of control, I began to cure myself of this compulsion. However, it still waits in the wings, ready to creep back whenever life seems particularly frenzied.

There are busier times and there are slower times in the academic calendar. When my husband was a professor, the changes in the pace of life on campus did not have much affect on our lives at home; I might well schedule family dental check-ups without giving a thought to what was going on at the college. But when your partner becomes a president or school head, the pace on campus becomes a large issue. In the opening months and again in the closing months of the academic year, the addition of even one simple task can seem a back-breaker. May, that month I used to think had the shortest name, I now call "that month in which I will not schedule anything that does not absolutely have to be done before the academic year ends". Now that I've learned to think of the very busiest months that way, living through them is easier.

Making Way for Down Time. Years ago a friend told me about her "three night rule". This was a woman whose husband was the newly-appointed pastor of a large urban congregation, and they had two young children. I think they could have dined out with members of their congregation or attended meetings or benefits every evening of every week, had they been so inclined. The "three night rule" was quite simple—any invitation which meant that the couple would be away from their children for three nights in a row was automatically refused.

I think leaders of academic institutions can easily justify a similar rule—recognizing, of course, that there will be strings of days when it's impossible to observe it. My friend was trying to save time for the family to be together, but that's not really my point here. I don't underestimate the need for that; family time is extremely important. But all of us also need an hour here or there when we can do next to nothing. Down time is when the machines are shut off for repair; it is not the same thing as time off. Down time can be that hour in the evening when you let your mind go quiet while tying fishing flies, playing the piano or watching television. It is a brief chance for the brain to repair itself by putting the day's business into proper perspective, while you concentrate ever so lightly on something else.

Unless there is some ongoing crisis, my husband and I screen all telephone calls in the evening. If callers leave a message, I listen to it and make a judgment about my husband's need to know right away. It took a couple of years for us to decide it was all right to do this. By that time we had had enough experience with evening callers to realize that we would have lost nothing except sleepless nights if we had screened the calls. The well-meaning person who telephones because he or she thinks you should know right now about something that's afoot may be over-reacting. Usually nothing can be done about it before morning anyway. In our house at the edge of campus we are never completely inaccessible. If there's a true emergency and a caller can't get through to us by telephone, he or she will probably think to call the security office or come over in person and knock on our door.

I *do* answer the doorbell in the evening but am always ready to say that my partner is working and I don't want to disturb him. I tend to be more curt than usual on these occasions; if the visitor takes away the impression that he or she dropped by at an inconvenient time, all the better.

Time on the Road. When traveling an academic leader is, to some extent, at the mercy of the staff members who schedule airline flights and appointments for those days on the road. One reason I insist on having a copy of my husband's full itinerary when he is leaving town is so that I can keep an eye on how hard he is being driven (or driving himself—he is often complicit to some degree in any over-scheduling during his travels). The pace set on these trips can easily creep up to the point that it's on the verge of breaking the traveler down. The people who set up the itinerary tend not to consider how air travel drains one's energy, how sitting in a taxi blocked in traffic, trying to get from one appointment to another, wears one out. They may not factor in the probable necessity for the leader to make phone calls during the day, calls back to campus to check in at the office and calls to transact other kinds of business. And they may not look at the total length of scheduled hours, remembering time-zone shifts, and ask themselves, "Can any human being operate at peak performance for so many hours on end?" So I do ask that question. When I see a day on an itinerary that begins with a 5 AM departure for the airport, is peppered throughout with taxi trips back and forth across some city, and ends with the start of a dinner engagement more than a dozen hours later, I weigh in. I ask the staff to take a close look at that itinerary, and I remind them that there needs to be some margin, in case there is a blow-up on campus or a sudden need to make numerous phone calls—or, heaven forbid, in case my husband has been ill or is a little run-down for some other reason.

Certainly there are times when the pace has to be set near the breaking point, and we recognize that. At other times, it is only when the travel itinerary is looked at in the context of the busy on-campus days before and after it that a problem becomes apparent. Oftentimes when travel arrangements and appointments are being made, the schedule for the on-campus days surrounding the trip is not firmed up. This is one way the overall pace, both on campus and off, comes to be relentless. How do you keep the overall balance, when the job is compartmentalized this way? Furthermore, my husband may be complicit, as I have said, wanting to make the most of his time in this or that city. But I know that he sometimes doesn't realize that the itinerary is packed too tightly until the evening before he leaves town. He simply has not had the opportunity to take a hard look at it. If he has given it his approval it has been on the basis of a quick scan, which he probably made while pre-occupied with the problem of finding time to pack his suitcase for the trip.

People who begin a conversation with, "I know how busy you are" are on the right track, but unless they've held a similar job, I am not sure they truly do understand what it's like for these academic leaders to be at the mercy of persistent, competing demands, day in and day out. Sure, one can always squeeze in the time for one more telephone conversation, one more brief meeting. But if the normal pace leaves a person utterly drained at the end of each day, there is no margin for the unexpected—an illness, a crisis on campus. And perhaps even worse, the joy goes out of the job, as the incumbent starts to count the days until he or she can retire from the fray.

The Male Point of View: "I can remember one day when I literally tried to book some time through [my wife's] secretary, for a meeting with her. We now have an interrupt rule. If I call [my wife's] office and ask to be put through to her, it happens."

6

Social Work, or Entertaining and Being Entertained

Let's Get Serious. When my husband changed careers our social life died; social *work* took its place. For most of the months of the year our official entertaining crowds out any thoughts of private entertaining. Many of the official functions we host are enjoyable, but we are always mindful that this kind of entertaining is a serious business.

With so much time and money channeled in this direction, it is worth the effort to consider how one might reap the most benefit from every event. Since Day One spouses have been sharing recipes and menu suggestions. That's the delicious part of this business, the icing on the cake. In this chapter I want to talk about the science of cake baking.

A dinner for six or eight people—where you can really get into an extended conversation with someone you find fascinating—*that* I have always enjoyed. But I never thought big, noisy cocktail parties were much fun. In our former life I would show up at such a party chiefly as an act of loyalty to the friend who was the host. I don't remember ever initiating, or even wanting to initiate, a party of that type. The thought of all the large parties we would be expected to host or attend was, for me, one of the scariest things about my husband's career change. So there is considerable irony in the fact that in midlife I chose to become a party planner.

My role as a party planner sprang from my wish to protect our home life, to bring into the planning process some consideration of the impact a proposed event might have on the family. I really got caught up in it when I realized what a shame it is when way too much food is prepared, or when an event misses its mark. I don't dread large parties any more; the thought of zillions of cut flowers which serve their purpose for only an hour or two is much more troubling to me.

I rarely apply myself to detailed menu planning; rather I think about the purpose of a proposed event and suggest formats that suit that purpose. The president or school head could think this through, but, in my experience, that doesn't happen. It's not a priority. The office staff is perfectly capable of planning events, of course; they may even enjoy doing it. They may have enough experience to know that a buffet dinner can be much less expensive than a cocktail reception. They may recognize that a sit-down dinner with a seating plan is the most expensive, complicated and time-consuming way to entertain. But they probably have not spent hundreds of hours observing parties, noting that one format serves a particular purpose much better than another. I make it my business to see that entertaining at the residence is effective—lest we have to have multiple parties, when one might have served.

If you are used to a rather quiet life, you may be stunned when you get a peek at what's ahead. When we were new I remember that the number of institutional functions we were expected to host each year was mind-boggling. I took it on trust that all the time, money and energy that went into this entertaining must be well-spent, or academic leaders all over the country wouldn't be doing it. Gradually I became somewhat inured. "Oh, another party? Sure, we can do that." After all, I wasn't doing the cooking or arranging the flowers. I had figured out how to get a conversation going with perfect strangers, so parties were less stressful for me. If some campus office thought we should throw a party, I was generally amenable to the suggestion. But I really surprised myself when I started proposing that additional parties be added to the schedule. I was the one who used to catch my breath when looking over the term's quota of functions.

I believe that even those of us who start with a Scrooge-like attitude eventually realize that hosting and attending official events is an extremely important part of the leader's job. Most of the functions my husband and I host serve either to welcome new members to the campus community, to thank those who have contributed in some way to the institution, or to mark an institutional rite of passage. In some instances we hope a party will give our guests an opportunity to get to know and to bond with each other. Sometimes it is an occasion for us to get acquainted with people who might become major contributors. No matter what the impetus for a party, you can bet that it is an opportunity for cultivation, for increasing the various kinds of support, from insiders and outsiders, that every institution needs.

Whether it's a reception in our home, elsewhere on campus or in a distant city, every event my husband and I host is a reflection on us, and each one is significant. Nevertheless, I do not wish to spend a significant chunk of my life planning events. Thus, for those functions which are not going to take place in our home, I usually opt out of the planning. We try to let staff know that these events matter to us, that we are ready to discuss any concerns, but we trust them to handle the arrangements. We hope that positive feedback, mentioning details we especially liked, will serve to keep staff aware that we do, indeed, care about the entertaining, that we are paying attention and appreciate their efforts.

Streamlining the Planning. Had someone asked me, eighteen years ago, what sort of tone I would like to set with our entertaining, I would have been completely flummoxed. No one asked, and in the beginning the functions we hosted were carbon copies of those our predecessors had hosted. That was probably the best way to streamline the planning during the deluge of those first months. But as we were able to focus attention on the entertaining, we started to change things in small ways that we thought would make events more comfortable, either for us or for our guests. I now see that we were, in making these changes, feeling our way to the tone that was right for us. These days I can describe it.

I can now give caterers and staff members some guidelines that will help them understand what kind of functions we like to host. For example, we want glassware and not plastic cups, unless the party is so large as to make this a real burden. We like to have a couple of flower arrangements scattered around, but not on every table and mantle. We like the menu to include some "healthy" hors d'oeuvres, good-tasting food without high fat content. We want several fruit juices offered along with the usual non-alcoholic beverage choices. As for liquor, we keep a list of "house" brands, which we use for most parties, and also a premium list for the really special events. We want experienced bartenders who have an aura of maturity about them. We will not hire college students as bartenders, even if they are trained and of legal age.

If we had entertained on a grander scale before my husband changed careers, if I had had prior experience with caterers, perhaps I would have been able to give these directives right off the bat. As it was, I had to learn how to design a large party that even I could enjoy.

Knowing what you want can help you get up to speed quickly, but there is, of course, no guarantee that it will be smooth sailing once you've stated your wishes. We have tried to avoid coming on too strong when we've been new, have tried to explain the "why" as well as the "what". Even so, we've been misunderstood. At one college students protested when they heard that student bartenders were unacceptable to us. While meeting with these students, my husband learned that they believed the ban was campus-wide. When he explained that the rule applied only to events in our home, and that students of legal age could continue to work behind the bar at the campus pub, they shrugged their shoulders and said, "Oh. No problem!"

Finding the Format That's Right for You. It is important to match the format of an event to its intended purpose; that should be an early and major consideration in planning any event. But the chosen format should also align well with the leader's style and family dynamics. It may take time to figure out this part of the equation, especially if you don't see yourself being particularly comfortable at *any* kind of event, but the effort pays off.

From functions that welcome new faculty and students at the opening of the year, through commencement week-end at the end, official entertaining tends to be similar from one campus to the next. Some event dates and details will be pretty well locked in before you arrive. I am guessing that, with a single nod of the head, plans for a year's worth of official entertaining could be snapped into place, *everything* done exactly as before. While this might be tempting, considering all the other decisions that have to be made during a leader's first few months, I don't think it is wise. It is very unlikely that what suited your predecessors will suit you in every way. Dates might not be flexible, but perhaps you can fiddle with locations and types of events. You may want to schedule more, or fewer, events at the residence. You may want to change the type of event. For example, if you are trying to preserve family life, an afternoon meeting with refreshments afterward might be substituted for what had traditionally been a dinner meeting.

Sometimes a dinner party which goes on and on until the last of the wine is finished is just exactly right for the occasion. Sometimes such a party is a nuisance. Engagements that go late (or *begin* late) in the evening can be real headaches for people who need to be at the top of their game the next day. It is especially difficult to extricate yourselves from a party that is going on too long when it is held in your home. After some aggravation in our first years we learned a few tricks.

If the occasion calls for both a cocktail hour and dinner, we sometimes schedule the dinner at a different location. A cocktail reception at the residence, followed by a dinner served elsewhere on campus, can be just as much of a treat for the guests—and we won't be caught, unable to excuse ourselves when we are ready to put an end to the evening. Occasionally we conspire to move guests along by scheduling something for them to do after dinner—providing tickets to a concert or play on campus, for example. Or we arrange for the party to continue elsewhere, with a set-up of coffee or after-dinner drinks at another location.

In trying to decide what sort of event to plan, I am conscious of certain trade-offs in time, effort and expense. While a buffet dinner may be easier to pull off and less expensive than a cocktail reception, it can entail twice as much in actual party time. A reception that is cocktails-only usually lasts an hour to an hour and a half. Guests often arrive all at once at official events, and if you have enough bartenders this is plenty of time to serve even a hundred of them. (Furthermore, my partner and I both want any function that requires standing on our feet to be kept under two hours; sessions longer than that risk back problems for both of us.) I figure a buffet dinner, served after allowing thirty minutes for guests to assemble, takes two hours; cocktails followed by a seated-and-served dinner takes three, at least. Toasts and speeches, of course, up the ante. In a week with several social events, even a half-hour difference in our time commitment becomes significant. At the planning stage we try to keep track of what sort of week we are building for ourselves.

It may seem cold and calculating to assign a designated number of hours to a particular type of event in this way. But I am mindful that it is easy to devalue one's time in the eyes of others by being *too* accessible—by entertaining the same group too frequently or at parties that go on too long. If, once in a while, guests feel they have not had as much access to my partner as they might have wished, I believe that that is defensible. There *should* be a premium on the leader's time.

The guests' time may also be at a premium, but they simply don't know how to make a graceful exit. This happens most often when we are entertaining students. My husband has a routine where he puts his hands on the table, starts to get up and says, "Well, this has been wonderful, but I'm sure you all have lots to do." I really don't think anyone feels as though they have been dismissed. On the contrary; they are likely to feel relief, because they were beginning to sense that the time for departure was near, but nobody wanted to be the one to break up the party.

Finding the Menu That's Right for the Guests. Our guests' dietary restrictions, food preferences, and food expectations are all matters we take very seriously. I have said that I don't get involved in detailed menu planning, but I always go over the menus in the planning stages, keeping some broad issues in mind. In looking over a proposed menu for a cocktail reception, I'll ask myself what any vegetarians or vegans will have to eat. Food allergies are a major concern, since it seems to me that the number of guests we host who are sensitive to nuts and/or shellfish is on the increase. If the Provost is allergic to shellfish, that doesn't mean we can't serve shellfish at any party s/he attends; but it does mean that our serving people have to know exactly what is in any particular hors d'oeu-vre so that they can answer guests' questions. Caterers are generally pretty sensi-tive to these matters.

For dinner parties where the numbers are smaller, we ask about dietary needs and restrictions ahead of time. The office staff keep records regarding individuals (such as that Provost) who turn up on numerous guest lists. If the dinner party is for people we don't know well, or at all, the staff ask very specific questions in the planning stages, letting the guests know what sorts of food (say, pork, lamb, fish) are under consideration, so that we won't plan a meal around something they can't eat or to which they have a strong aversion.

Dinners at the official residence can be popular items on the auction lists, when local non-profits have benefit auctions. Several times a year we offer a din-ner party for four or six guests, rotating the offer through various charities. Often the winning bidders are people we have never met, so the food preference/allergy questions must be asked. I tend to get a little more involved in planning menus for these occasions, because I want to make sure that the guests go away feeling they got about what they expected out of the evening. Frequently the benefit din-ner is their first visit to the official residence and may be the only opportunity they will have. Something that could be considered "comfort food" or in any way construed as a "stew" is probably not a good choice, no matter how much the caterer assures me that it will be unforgettable and beyond wonderful.

Keeping the Upper Hand. Living in an official residence, we certainly expect to accommodate a good deal of entertaining. However, I think a few boundaries are in order to buoy up awareness that this is a *home*, and to avoid too much wear and tear on the house, or the staff who work the parties that happen there. I know cases where the official residence is considered just another venue on cam-pus, a place where any group can hold an event. I cannot imagine making my home in any place that was *that* available. Such an expectation would be a deal-breaker for us; my personal space is too important to me.

Staff members who schedule events at the official residence often don't realize how much time is needed for setting up beforehand, and for breaking down and cleaning up afterward. When we have a dinner party for more than a dozen, it's necessary to move the regular furniture out of some of the rooms to make way for folding tables and chairs. I prefer to schedule the set-up on the day before the party and the break-down the day after; otherwise the help would have to arrive much earlier and stay much later. That means that a sizeable dinner party takes over our house for about 48 hours. If there's a compelling reason, we can compress this time to make room for another event. In general, however, I don't want to push our entertaining help that hard. So if someone asks if we might have "just a little dinner party" the day before the big one, I'm likely to resist.

We have made it clear at our various posts that we do not wish to host functions in our home on Saturdays or Sundays if we can possibly avoid it. Often those who plan the schedule for major events like reunion week-end don't really care whether a party at the residence happens on a Friday or a Saturday. But it makes a big difference for those living in the house. Any time there is an event held in our home it means a day full of noise and bustle, deliveries and interruptions. If the residence can be kept fairly peaceful on the Saturday and Sunday of a busy week-end, we will be less drained. A half-hour of rest stolen in a quiet house before you go off to Saturday night's party on campus can be priceless. Sometimes it can't be worked out, but it certainly does not hurt to ask to be accommodated in this matter if possible.

It is easy to be misunderstood when you're talking about making changes. I once had an alumna, whom I had barely met, say to me, "I hear you don't entertain on Saturdays." She was a hard-working volunteer, and I can understand why, if that was *all* that she had heard, she might have been peeved. Again, it is important to be clear about the "why" as well as the "what".

My basic rule is "family needs trump entertaining needs". I think it would be pretty difficult for anyone to argue against that as a rule of thumb. Once, when we were living in an old-style mausoleum, I started thinking in the midst of a reunion week-end how different the schedule would have to be if we still had children living at home. Three large receptions were held at our house in the course of two days. The kitchen was pulsing with caterers for many hours each day, and catering equipment was left on the counters overnight between events. It was just about impossible for me to prepare the evening meal. Some of the food in the refrigerators was "ours" and some was "theirs", but I was the only one in the house who knew which was which.

If we had children living at home I would have guarded against a schedule such as this, particularly near the end of the academic year, when the whole family is more than a little weary of household disruptions. We would have planned to either combine events or change the venue of some. Since our children are grown I now allow this kind of scheduling. My husband and I aren't afraid to wade through the caterers if we want a snack, and we bat away minor irritations because we realize that they are the result of decisions we made in the planning stage.

Communicating the Party Plan. For years I had meetings with caterers at which we discussed the upcoming event and went over the plans in detail. We talked about the menus, the placement of food tables and bars, number of bartenders needed, flower arrangements and so on, and the caterer took notes and made sketches. I had in my head the idea that I ought to be able to show up moments before a party was to begin and find that everything was just as we had planned it. But when I tried to do that, I sometimes walked into a jumble. Tables weren't where they were supposed to be, our guests couldn't get at, or away from, the bar, and garbage cans were in full view. I concluded that I just had to be on hand to direct the staff when set-up began.

Many caterers copy the notes they take in a planning session onto an order sheet, which contains the food order as well as templates for table and chair set-ups. For years I never saw a single order sheet and didn't know such a thing existed. How much trouble I could have saved myself if I had! Order sheets had been available all along but weren't being widely distributed. The department that was delivering folding tables, chairs, trash barrels and so forth didn't know the plan. When the catering crew arrived to drape the tables and found them in unexpected places, they probably assumed I had changed the set-up. If I had asked for a copy of the completed order sheet, one I could post at the residence, I would have been freed up on party day.

Communication with the grounds crew is also vital when events are scheduled at the residence. The grounds department is likely to anticipate your having guests in the course of major week-ends on campus and may come and spiff up the grounds without being asked. But they can hardly be expected to know about each and every function scheduled for the residence throughout the year. In those spring days, when your lawn needs mowing at least once a week, sooner or later they are going to arrive with their noisy equipment in the middle of your luncheon party. I try to avoid this kind of annoyance by making sure the grounds supervisor knows our entertaining schedule well ahead of time. He can then make sure that any work that's needed has been done before an event begins. If the grounds crew takes pride in keeping things looking trim, they will be grateful for the warning you give them.

Mixing with the Crowds. In the beginning the exhaustion I regularly felt after huge parties and big campus week-ends led me to begin dreading the prospect of these events. Even though I knew I would meet some fascinating people and begin to make new friends, I often had to really buck myself up to face the crowd. The physical effort didn't amount to much more than standing or sitting, and it didn't seem like I was working *that* hard at making conversation and getting to know people. The draining power of these events was something of a mystery. Then I read in the newspaper a comment made by Princeton researcher J. Nicole Shelton: "When you have to control your behavior, it takes a lot of energy." That is surely part of the explanation. My husband and I are both controlling our behavior every moment during an event, aware that we are playing ambassador for the institution. We are also pre-occupied with making it a positive occasion for everyone. In addition, for me, the whole idea of these events goes against my grain. It's not the sheer number of people; I love walking down a crowded sidewalk in Manhattan. But making my way through a crowd with my nametag carefully pinned on my lapel, starting up fleeting conversations one after another—that behavior does not come naturally. At a large party where I am not "on duty" as a hostess and there is little if any connection to our institution, you will find me hunkered down in a corner somewhere having a lengthy conversation with one or two people, not flitting about like a butterfly.

I learned early on to pace myself physically on the day before a large reception, so my back could take the hours of standing. I had not, however, thought about the need to reserve my social energy during the time before the party. When we were first starting out I tried to mix with the crowd all day long on major weekends. That's what my husband was doing, and I figured if he could do it, so could I. But by party time in the afternoon or evening I sometimes felt like getting in the car and leaving town. Now I reserve my social energy during these times, picking and choosing where to show up, so that when guests start arriving at our house I can smile and greet them with more sincerity.

My husband and I usually split up to work receptions and parties. As I noted in an earlier chapter, I arm myself with information about the guests ahead of time. If the evening includes a sit-down dinner after a reception, I want to know who I'll be sitting with so I won't spend much time chatting over cocktails with the people who will be my dinner partners. If personnel from the alumni or development office are among the guests, we sometimes ask them to be watchful during the event and help us out in certain ways. If you are having a hard time getting away from a guest, a staff member can interrupt and whisk you off to meet someone else without seeming too ungracious. And staff can hustle guests when it's time to move on to dinner, or when the hour has come for the party to end.

Making Notes after an Event. Much of the official entertaining is repeated annually in pretty much the same form. It's good to make notes shortly after events, about ways in which the plan might be improved, with the hope that guests will get more enjoyment out of it the next time around. Notes such as "Rainy day—group too big to entertain indoors—need to designate rain site"; "Large group, short cocktail hour—limit to wine/beer to expedite bar service"; and "Chocolate-glazed cookies melted in the sun" will remind you of details you might not otherwise recall when it's time to plan this same party next year.

Evaluating the Caterer. Of course you want the food to be good, and to be served with style. You want value for the dollar and some variety and novelty in the offerings. You need the caterers to be dependable, and it's great if they are so likable that you enjoy having them in your home. Having had no personal experience with caterers before my husband's career change, I would have thought that about covered the criteria. But I now know there are two more issues, the "before" and the "after" behavior.

Caterers range from those who whisk into your home an hour before the party, with most of the food already prepared, to those who do much of the food preparation at your house, starting several hours before the party. I think it is fair to ask a caterer what you might expect in this regard, so that you can consider how the family might be affected.

The "after" behavior can be trickier. We have had caterers who leave behind garbage, sticky floors and dirty ovens. Perhaps they assume that our kitchen, like the cafeterias on campus, is cleaned every day. It isn't. At the other end of the spectrum we have had some caterers who do a good job with the clean-up but take so long that my husband and I are positively aching for them to be gone so we can go to bed. This may be simply a problem of sensitivity. The crew may be accustomed to letting up their pace once the guests leave. When they are working in dining halls and campus kitchens rather than in someone's home, they don't inconvenience anyone when they take their time finishing up their job. A few words to the head of the crew, indicating that you will want to lock up for the night or let the children into the kitchen as soon as possible, might help.

The caterer you are probably going to want to hang on to is the one who asks you, a day or two after the party, "Was everything just as you wished?"

A Final Word. People who love big parties or who have a natural gift for entertaining will, I hope, find some tips they can use in this chapter. But if, like me, you are not a party person and even reading about them makes you squirm, here's a thought. If your guests are honestly enjoying themselves, you might find the feeling is contagious. And without a doubt, it is exhilarating to arrive at the end of an event and realize that your carefully-laid plans worked really, really well. The satisfaction found in those moments is what keeps me going.

The Male Point of View: "One thing that drove me away from attending some events was the irritation when we were standing together being introduced as 'the President and ...', and as soon as 'the President' was uttered the person being introduced turned to me and extended a hand. It never bothered [my wife], or so she says, but it really got under my skin after a while."

7

Marriage and Spousework

My husband and I both abhor the current craze in the media for revealing the most intimate facts about personal relationships. We consider our marriage a very private matter, and we don't discuss it with others. At the same time, it is no secret that these leadership positions shake up marriages, and the specifics, I would be willing to bet, are pretty universal.

Years ago there was a cartoon circulating among school heads and their spouses. It was a familiar type, featuring a couple in bed, but there was a twist. The woman was trying to sleep, but the man was reading from a file folder. One whole wall of the bedroom was filled floor to ceiling with file drawers, several of them hanging open. The caption, to the best of my memory, read: "But honey, you knew when you married me that I wanted to be a headmaster."

Some of us knew our partners wanted to be school heads or college presidents, and some of us didn't. But even those of us who knew still may not have had much of an idea what such a job might entail, for both the leader and the spouse.

Of the many female spouses I've known—and I limit this observation to women because I simply have not encountered enough male spouses to make any judgment about them—those who seem most content with their situation have this in common: they are honestly willing to let their husbands' careers dominate their lives. For the most part these women have put their personal careers aside, for a while at least. In one case the situation was a little different. This woman told me that she had always known that her husband was a workaholic and that his job would come before their marriage. She married him anyway.

Spouses who are not quite so content sometimes live in a state of perpetual exasperation. They are exasperated with the monster-job and not their partners, but their partners are so closely identified with their jobs that there is plenty of room for tangled thinking. Straightening out tangled thinking when so much emotion is involved is no small task. I don't believe it's possible for a couple to give too much time to the effort.

The most daunting challenge for a leadership couple is finding time to nurture their relationship. How can you separate from this oversized job, put all the pressing problems out of mind, and really get away from it all? This might be more important for your marriage than it ever was before, even as the things you used to enjoy doing together no longer fit the bill. It can be hard even to find a restaurant where you can dine together quietly, without people who recognize you continually stopping by your table.

Watching the varsity game or attending the school concert morphs into work instead of play. You are on display in such settings, and some part of your brain wants to be thinking of matters like what you are going to say to the coach or the orchestra conductor afterward. On rare occasions a performance is so magical that you can lose yourself in it, but it takes stronger magic these days.

You really have to work at making time to be together, and it never gets any easier to do. You have to plan ahead and then be ready to change plans at the last moment. After all these years, I know when my husband is pre-occupied; I don't think he can fool me. When we have a week coming up that looks as though it might allow a break, we might start talking on Monday or Tuesday about what we could do together on the week-end. Then we see how the week unfolds. If something truly serious (as opposed to the recurrent nagging worries) blows up, then our outing might be doomed. By Friday night or Saturday morning, my husband is likely to know whether he is going to be able get his mind off his job for a few hours. I will probably know as well. If it is not going to be a refreshing, relaxing time for both of us, it is no good. So we renegotiate. We try to find another time, in the not-too-distant future, when we can go off for a few hours and just enjoy each other's company.

Even though we are both aware of the need, sometimes there are long stretches between opportunities. On those week-ends when my husband can hardly get away from his desk, one thing that makes a big difference for me is this: he is at least in the house, at work in his home office. I am hard-pressed to explain why the fact that he is at home, and not at his campus office, means so much to me. He is behind a closed door, glued to his chair, working away; I am working at my own desk or around the house, trying to keep things fairly quiet. This is not exactly quality time together. Perhaps it's a sense of "us against the world", but with more coziness and comfort than that phrase suggests.

I used to have regular commitments that took me away from home in the evenings. I now have almost none. I have a sort of standing appointment every evening—to spend time with my husband if he is at home. Yes, this is every bit as lop-sided as it sounds. Now that our children are grown, I spend a lot of time alone. I don't mean to sound pathetic—remember, I am by nature a solitary person. It's just that I have yet to discover a better way to keep in touch with my partner.

I have actually explained my reluctance to join clubs and committees in these terms, my need to be available, and I find that people understand readily. But by "standing appointment" I don't mean to imply that this is a time when we discuss our personal issues. Evenings are often the worst times for deliberate discussions, because one or both of us may be already feeling strung out. These evenings are times when the chief goal is to be in the same room with each other, reading the newspapers and talking about the day's experiences. In our former lives we took such evenings for granted; now we prize them.

On occasion I decline an invitation to join my husband at a campus event, and I forego his company when I could have been with him. Usually the event is something such as a dinner which an academic department is hosting for a guest lecturer. My rule of thumb is that if the spouses of the other guests are not invited, I will not attend even if I am invited. Spouses of other guests may be left out because of budget constraints, or because the point of the event is not entirely social. Sometimes I opt out of attending a party my husband is hosting in our own home. A dinner party given with the nominal purpose of thanking a committee for its work may actually be one inspired by the wish to nudge the members of the group toward closer bonds with each other. My presence can be a hindrance, changing the social dynamic for the part of the group I'm seated with.

We both understand that my decision to stay away is not a rejection. It is not that I prefer to be alone or engaged in my own pursuits, but my presence at such events is not going to add much of anything and might even be a distraction. There was a time when I would drag myself to some event I really did not want to attend, to some function where I knew I would feel out of place, thinking, "If *he* can do it, *I* can do it." It seemed to me then that I was supporting my husband by going along. But that grudging behavior probably contributed to the bitterness and resentment I felt in those years. Better that I pick and choose, and go along only when I can feel quite sure that, afterward, I will be glad I participated.

For us as a couple, decision-making doesn't happen in the same way. I have become more self-reliant. We used to spend time discussing a lot of things, such as whether we should consider replacing a major appliance. As our income grew over the years of our marriage, we continued to do this more out of habit than need. In the face of all the decisions my husband now makes each day, that kind of discussion seems too insignificant to bother with. So these days I operate more independently. In part this is a natural response to the small amount of time we have together; what there is, I want to maintain as quality time.

When there's something that we really do need to discuss, I bide my time when possible, waiting for a good opportunity to introduce the matter. I deal with it on my own, until I think my husband can give it good attention. This does not mean that he is opting out of family decisions, or that the institution has taken priority over life at home. All it means is that my partner can rely on me to carry on alone, when necessary, to the best of my ability.

I sometimes wonder what we would be like, as a married couple, if my husband had not changed careers. I wonder if we would know and understand each other so well. I don't think we would. You form a team when you need a team.

The Male Point of View: "[A male spouse] has to be aware that his wife's image of him might be messed up for a while, because he is no longer the man he was, before he quit his life, picked up and moved with her."

8

Things Our Children Taught Us

I would never want anyone to make any parenting decision based on what little I know. The stakes are just too high; I don't want that responsibility! However, if you have children, you are likely to have some concerns regarding them. Some things I've learned from my experiences might be worth your reading about.

When we were preparing to move to the town where my husband held his first leadership post, we needed to decide where to enroll our daughter in school. Since she was at the beginning of her middle-school years, she was clearly not going to be attending the institution my husband was invited to lead, which was a high school. The town, small as it was, afforded an independent-school choice for our daughter, but we did not even make a visit there because we were from the outset leaning toward the public school system for several reasons. Chief among them was that it would be the easiest transition for our child—no small consideration, realizing the many ways in which her life was about to change. Also, the whole family would get to know more members of the community that way. We expected to move our daughter into an independent school eventually, but not right away. It turned out to be a good decision, and one which we would make again.

At the time we felt no pressure to choose one school over the other, not from the institution my husband was to head, or from any other institution, or from any townspeople. The matter never came up. So I was taken back some months later when a resident of the town, someone I barely knew, asked me point-blank, "Why did you put your daughter in the public school?" She may have asked that question of every family that made a similar choice, but I doubt it. This was my first clue that our parenting decisions were now in the public domain.

The way children react to the peculiarities of this life depends on their stage of development, so I've incorporated into this chapter experiences from the time we moved into our first official residence, through our child-raising years and even beyond. Our daughter was ten years old when my husband became a headmaster, and our son was eighteen and setting off for college. Moving to a new town was not very hard on either child, especially since we kept the house that had formerly been our home and returned to it regularly during summer vacations.

In the beginning our daughter was flattered when the students, who were all at least four years older, paid attention to her. She was one of the items on the students' scavenger hunt during our first year, and she thought that was pretty neat. But as Kate grew older the attention was not so welcome. At the boarding school many faculty members brought their families to the dining hall for supper each night; it was considered a good thing for them to be there. My husband and I tried to eat supper there at least once a week, schedules permitting. We always tried to choose a table where there were some students we didn't know very well. Our daughter came along quite happily at first, but as the years went by she started to resist. From the conversations that polite students tried to make with Kate it was clear that they basically knew one thing about her—that she rode horses. It no doubt grew tedious to have this one topic brought up again and again, but other issues gradually came into play: the growing self-consciousness that was natural for a child of her age, and the fact that she was almost as old as the high school students and sometimes felt patronized. My husband and I continued to eat in the dining hall occasionally, but we stopped pressuring Kate to join us.

When our daughter was a teen-ager, she taught us a lesson about family time. It came about because of the inevitable temptation for school heads or presidents to combine a little business with the family vacation. It sometimes helps financially (the institution foots part of the vacation bill), but even more tempting is the thought that visiting that alumnus while on holiday in Florida will make a second trip unnecessary. It seems like the family wins in the end, since Mom or Dad doesn't have to be away so much.

It sounds good put that way, but that may not be the way the child sees it. What our daughter saw was that a significant part of the family trip had been planned around some people she didn't know, and we were expecting her not only to tag along but to be on her best behavior—polite, smiling and acting as though she were enjoying herself. She was having none of it. We had done something of the kind a few years before, mixing business with the family vacation, and got away with it. But this time our daughter was old enough to recognize her rights and demand them. It was an embarrassing situation for my husband and me, but we knew in our hearts that we could not blame the child. It was the last time we ever let business creep into anything we billed as a family trip.

We were just into our second year in the new job when our son came home from college for the week-end, on rather short notice. Since the upcoming Monday was a holiday, I didn't think this was at all strange. I blithely assumed that he just wanted to get away from the city, to come back to the hills for a breather.

We had a houseguest that week-end, an alumnus who was a school guest, someone we didn't know very well. That meant that my husband and I were "on" all week-end, and neither of us paid close attention to our son's state of mind when he came home. He seemed fine. Well, he wasn't fine. He went through two full days, needing to talk to us but not having the chance. It was late on Sunday evening before the story came out—late enough that my husband and our guest had already gone to bed. By the time my son and I finished talking it was past midnight.

It is a shame that something like that had to happen before I realized that I was taking my children's well-being for granted. Overall I feel absolutely sure that our children gained more than they lost when their father changed careers, but there is no doubt in my mind that, in parts of those first years, they lost some parental attentiveness.

When you are new and meeting hundreds of people, many of them express an interest in your children. I believe it is good to think about boundaries for talking about the children, and to think about this ahead of time, before you are under pressure to make conversation with strangers. You might consult any pre-teen and teen-age children, to see how they feel about your giving out a little information about them when people ask. This empowers them to some extent and may open valuable lines of communication. These boundaries may have to change as the children grow older.

Children need to understand that information about them will travel and mutate in the same way that information about you and your partner will do. The whole family is vulnerable to this. Treating the rumor mill as something of interest rather than concern, seeing and sharing the humor when funny permutations come to light, can foster a healthy attitude and help to diffuse the pressure children might feel. You can't control the rumors, but you might be able to turn them into something that knits the family closer together.

One of the most important things I have learned is that when parents are over-stressed children sometimes pay the price. Sensitive children can pick up on their parents' stress and might even believe that they are the cause of it. This happens even after children are grown up and out of the nest. Communication, communication, communication! We all know how important this is, but it is easy to let it slide when we think we are managing to hide the tension, to keep it out of family life. Children may not be able to understand why the stress is there, even if you were to explain it to them—which you probably are not able, or free, to do. But at least you will have given them to understand that they are not part of the problem.

My husband had already developed good relationships with our son and daughter before he changed careers; that was something that we needed to maintain but did not have to build from scratch. Luckily, our children share some of their father's passions. I am happy to see them off on their father-son fishing trips or their father-daughter 15K races, to wave good-bye and stay behind, pondering how fortunate we are.

The Male Point of View: Being unemployed, I threw myself into community service and raising our son, who was still in high school. Taking over as the "primary" parent led to a wonderful experience and a much richer relationship.

9

Pay for the Spouse—Yes or No?

It's the Thought That Counts. I was offered a stipend in 1989 when my husband became a headmaster, and I accepted it gratefully. Because I had given up a paid job to move to this new campus and because I intended to focus my energy on the spouse role instead of an outside job, it seemed perfectly natural for the pay to be offered, and for me to accept it. That the amount was modest and the institution wealthy probably fostered my heedlessness. In time I learned that monetary compensation for spouses is not the norm for female spouses, and is nearly unheard-of for male spouses. A recent survey by the Council of Independent Colleges (2004) revealed that less than 25% of the spouses who responded were receiving any compensation. Shortly thereafter the Association of American Universities estimated that about half of its member institutions pay something to the leader's spouse.

I now also know that not all the spouses who are offered pay wish to accept it; in fact, there's quite a discussion going on. An article in the *New York Times* in January of 2003 reported on the growing trend of paying spouses, and on the arguments of spouses who are for and against such pay. Those for and those against pay have this in common: they all claim to be both progressive and feminist. When that sort of controversy surrounds a topic, those of us who accept pay should expect that we might well be called upon to justify our decision. The newspaper article concluded with a comment from one spouse, a woman who had accepted the money that was offered but was burned for it in the school newspaper. I would second her advice, which was "it has to be dealt with by each individual person."

At our current post I receive an honorarium at the end of each academic year. I have come to value the remuneration I receive not for the actual dollars but for what they symbolize: that the board of trustees acknowledges me as a contributor to my husband's efforts. My husband has now served three different boards. Before any of the boards decided to offer me remuneration, they must have considered the situation of the leader's spouse. It pleases me to think that at some point in time these boards gave some thought to the matter. I believe that it would benefit trustee/partner relationships if any board that was seeking a new academic leader discussed the pay-for-spouses issue, whether or not they decided to offer remuneration. In the process trustees would surely learn more about the kinds of contributions spouses make and the effects that the leaders' jobs have on the leaders and their families.

The Representational Role. There is one aspect of the spouse's role that is inescapable, and even those who are least actively involved will find it hard to dodge. I refer to the representational role, being a living logo of the institution.

Many of us are startled to realize how this representational role is going to change our lives, and in particular our relationships with other people. We find that we may, indeed, be free to choose how to be involved, but that is not the same thing as freedom from any sort of responsibility toward the institution. The representational role can limit the employment possibilities for the spouse. Some in less urban areas have found it very difficult, if not impossible, to find jobs because of perceptions that there would somehow be a conflict of interest.

Board members who have experience as corporate leaders, or as the partners of corporate executives, will have some grasp of what the representational role might entail, but I would maintain that it is more of a burden for partners of academic leaders than for those of corporate leaders. Perhaps it is because education's "product" is people. If my husband ran a manufacturing firm, whether it produced paper clips or jet engines, I would not expect to be constantly assessed as an indicator of the quality or desirability of that product. If the public didn't like my behavior, my personality or my politics, no matter; none of that would have any bearing on the product's intrinsic value. As the wife of a college president, I think about how I present myself to the public all the time. I may not choose to be an active ambassador for the institution my partner heads; nevertheless, I am inevitably seen as a representative of it by proxy. I have a responsibility to my husband, and through him to the institution, to do nothing that will cause harm. If I don't pay attention to that fact, I can cause all sorts of trouble.

The institutional community and perhaps the civic community will have ideas about what constitutes appropriate behavior for the spouse. If I'm running errands in a rush and let the door slam in someone's face, a quick "Sorry" is not enough. I have just withdrawn a penny from the account, the account in which outsiders' good feelings toward the institution, and their good opinion of the people associated with it, are collected. If I run those errands after my gym class, still wearing my sweatsuit, tongues will wag. And this may be true even though the streets are peppered with people in athletic attire. You may cry, "Unfair!"—but that's the way it is. It's worth noting that small acts of kindness and courtesy also have big echoes.

There is no real hardship in society's expectation that the spouse's behavior will be within the bounds of propriety. But those boundaries are not marked, and that makes the representational role more of a burden. It is tiring to be constantly second-guessing yourself, wondering if you said or did the right thing. And sometimes the spouse realizes what it means to be a living logo rather late, after causing a problem that could have been avoided.

The partner of a newly-appointed leader needs to consider this aspect of his or her situation, and the sooner the better. I believe it would benefit everyone involved if the board had a candid discussion with the spouse of the leader-to-be, acknowledging that board members are powerless to free partners from this representational role and indicating their intention to be supportive and understanding.

By including a discussion of the representational role in this chapter, I do not mean to imply that spouses should be paid for making the efforts we all make in this area. Personally, I find the perks of the position sufficient compensation for what is, after all, simply an expectation that I will behave in a seemly manner. Though I think about this constantly, as I have said, it does become second nature after a while. It is because of the confusion that roils around the topic of spousal compensation that I raise this topic here. I believe spouses and trustees should consider all angles of the spouse's experience and sort out just what parts of it might justify compensation of some type.

On the one occasion I took outside employment in the community where my husband was posted I did not run into the conflict-of-interest problems that some spouses report. If I had, I would surely feel that the representational role was a serious obstacle; perhaps, in that case, I would also feel entitled to some financial compensation for being caught in such a predicament.

Task Sharing. The contributions that partners make, by being always aware of their responsibility to their mates and the institutions they lead, cannot be weighed and measured. The value of other sorts of contributions is more easily assessed. If a spouse is going to be involved in things like overseeing the care of an official residence, planning events, entertaining the trustees' spouses—tasks which an institution often pays someone else to do when the leader has no spouse or has a spouse who is not going to assume those chores—it seems to me there can be no question that remuneration of the spouse is a legitimate expense. In fact, paying the spouse and thereby giving him or her a *bona fide* position on the staff can avoid the problems some of us run into, when we work closely with institutional employees who don't feel we have a right to make suggestions or requests.

Some spouses will not wish to have a salary even for tasks like these because, while they are willing to do the work, they don't want anyone to expect it of them. They want to feel free to refuse requests and decline invitations. And there are many other reasons for choosing to remain unpaid. A spouse at an institution that is financially strapped might feel uncomfortable accepting a salary. At a state-supported institution annual evaluations may be required, and the spouse might not welcome that inspection. Some partners don't want to be paid unless pay is also offered to others who perform similar functions, the partners of deans and department heads, for example. Some spouses wish to keep their contribution on a strictly volunteer basis, because of the message that sends about the importance of volunteerism. Of course, others believe that that kind of volunteerism is a yoke which society once put on women's shoulders, something which we should resist; they want to be paid because the money gives validity to the way they spend their time. And a spouse may also have an eye on the *curriculum vitae*. Taking time out of the paid workforce for a stint of unpaid spousework will leave a gap on the resume. Whether the spouse is male or female, gaps on resumes always raise questions in the minds of future employers. And when society in general understands so little about what spouses do, and why time out might be important, even necessary, it is not easy to make people understand one's choice to take leave from paid employment.

Forms of Compensation. Beyond the discussion of the pros and cons of remuneration is the consideration of size and type. Compensation need not be an actual salary that comes monthly, or an honorarium that comes as a lump sum at the end of the academic year. It could come in the form of an annuity. For a spouse who plans to be actively involved in the life of the surrounding community, the institution might pay membership fees in local service clubs and nonprofit organizations. A spouse who lets it be known that he or she is willing to participate in such groups is likely to be invited, even urged, to join all kinds of organizations. Some of them will be of more interest than others, yet rejecting those of less appeal can create an awkward situation. In our former lives I became a card-carrying member of an organization only when I was ready to pledge myself to active participation; I didn't join up unless I was truly interested. But many organizations will want the cachet of having local leaders—and their spouses—on the membership lists. This is part of being a living logo. While the institution might pay the president's membership fee in a service club just to show support for a worthy organization, it might not occur to anyone to offer that same perk to the spouse, who may receive as many, or more, invitations to join local groups.

Compensation could come in the form of a personal expense account to cover things like costs, including child care, when the partner travels with the leader. It could even be a clothing budget. Don't laugh! As one partner noted in *The President's Spouse, Volunteer or Volunteered* (published by the National Association of State Universities and Land-Grant Colleges, 1984), we are often "drawn into the company of the invariably well dressed". In the same book David Riesman raised the possibility of a clothing allowance. Our social calendars demand big wardrobes, and travel wreaks havoc on them. I spent more time and money shopping for clothes in my first few years of spousework than I want to think about.

"Pay or no pay" may not be a question that has to be answered, once and for all, at the very beginning of things. However, when pay is offered it means the door is open to a spouse to negotiate some type of monetary compensation at some point. This is truly an issue you have to decide for yourself, and yet I can't help giving a little advice. It's just the cautionary advice that might be given to anyone entering new territory: Don't burn your bridges. The trend is definitely in the direction of more spouses accepting compensation. The perks that go with the position can be terrific, but there are many trade-offs. For all kinds of reasons, you might find yourself wishing later on that you had remained open to the idea of accepting some form of compensation.

The Male Point of View: I gave up a faculty position to move with my wife. There was no place for me [at the new university], and the loss of income was a problem.

10

The Future of Spousework

The Endangered List. The most fundamental kind of spousework, just like housework, will never go away. It comes with the territory when you share your life with an academic leader. And as long as we spouses are seen as living logos of the institutions our partners serve, we will need to adapt our behavior in certain ways. We are not pledged to *serve*, but it is, and always will be, incumbent on us to *preserve* the good name of the institution.

With regard to the other types of spousework—the artful kind, which implies supporting the leader in a skillful, intelligent way, and the active kind, which implies a significant commitment of time—the future may not be so secure. Artful, intelligent spousework, for me and for many others, is the good stuff. It is complex and challenging, and the work can become its own reward. It is what some of us instinctively hoped for, even if we couldn't exactly define it. It is what we searched for until we discovered it, or it discovered us. And that's the problem. Though this kind of spousework has been around a long time, it remains a quiet, unrecognized achievement. I have no doubt that some people wrap up their years in the spouse's role without ever suspecting that there was a whole level of spousework they never glimpsed.

Any spouse can attain the level of artful spousework with some perseverance. In the past the traditional spouse was a woman who was pretty well locked into her role, whether or not she enjoyed it or was any good at it. The options that spouses have today, from personal careers to divorce, simply were not available or were beyond the pale. Those spouses of the past did not have much choice but to persevere, and many of them, no doubt, broke through to meaningful spousework. Today spouses can walk away, in either a figurative or a literal sense. At the same time, I believe intelligent spousework is more important than ever before because the leaders' jobs have become more demanding, and those demands press ever harder on their families. We need to be introducing spouses to the possibilities inherent in their positions. We need to be offering some serious mentoring, support that goes beyond recipe exchanges and entertaining tips and a well-meaning pat on the back.

About active spousework, I am even less sanguine. Personal career choices will always impinge on active spousework. Fair enough, I say. More problematic is the lingering culture of expectation. Some decades ago a sociologist named Hanna Papanek coined a phrase, "the two-person single career" (*American Journal of Sociology*, vol. 78, no. 4, pp. 852-872). The two-person single career is a "combination of formal and informal institutional demands which is placed on both members of a married couple of whom only the man is employed by the institution." You would think that the women's movement would have killed this phenomenon dead by now. Not so. The "formal and informal institutional demands" still lurk in the corners.

At many institutions today, search committees and boards of trustees assure incoming spouses that their active participation will not be taken for granted. But there can be problems with these assurances. Some of us find that expectations are still harbored elsewhere. The word that spouses are free to choose hasn't yet reached all of the campus's stakeholders; their attitudes are conditioned by their experiences with spouses from the past—perhaps a very distant past, in the case of older alumni. Recently I have met people, members of one constituency or another, who expressed surprise that I had chosen to be "involved"; they honestly did not expect it. But that liberated attitude, though refreshing, is still exceedingly rare. In addition to the problem of lingering expectations there is the fact that some spouses still feel pressed to take on unwanted tasks. Many leaders find there is simply not enough support staff to help take care of the house and/or the entertaining load that come with the job. They may not have time to run their personal errands or to help with family responsibilities. Spouses step into the gap, sometimes with reluctance; they become actively involved under duress.

Expectations—the kind that weren't supposed to be around any more—can make us feel trapped, particularly if they are ones we really don't want to fulfill. Quite naturally, we want to escape. Sometimes escape seems too complicated, causing more trouble than it might be worth, so we cave in. I have done this many times, but not so readily now that I recognize that, by doing so, I am helping to perpetuate the culture of expectation. I am only making it harder for the person who might follow me. How we spouses deal with the lingering culture of expectation will have an impact on the future of spouses' participation.

When unwanted expectations are a problem and saying "no" doesn't seem to be an option, some spouses find ways of taking themselves off the available list. They take new jobs or throw themselves more completely into their own careers.

They may decide to live separately. Other kinds of difficulty can also cause spouses to veer away from active involvement in their partners' careers. An official residence that affords little comfort or privacy, the realization that their partners are not going to have much time to share with them in the foreseeable future, feelings of isolation—these things also drive spouses to look for solutions that, in the end, take them away from active involvement. Some of these coping mechanisms, while helpful, are band-aids applied to problems that need to be addressed. Even worse, a particular solution may address one problem while it creates another, and in the final analysis it is not always clear that there has been any net gain. And when spouses make deliberate efforts to distance themselves from institutional life because of some discomfort with the situation in which they find themselves, the institutions themselves are diminished.

Personally, I remain committed to an active role. I help with the entertaining and the management of the residence. I show up at all kinds of functions on campus and accompany my husband on some of his travels. I do my homework before I meet new members of the various constituencies. I stay involved in these ways even though it cuts into the time I might devote to my own interests. I stay involved even though I am an introvert who would rather curl up with a good book than attend an event. I stay involved even though it irritates me when I am treated like a non-entity or a figurehead. I do it to help my husband. I do it so we will be closer as a couple. Somewhere in my brain the pros and cons, with regard to my own well-being, are under continual, if unconscious, assessment. The positive experiences that have accrued from active spousework continue to outweigh the tedious and unpleasant ones. I know that if I had dropped out years ago, as I once was sorely tempted to do, I would have missed many wonderful friendships, many memorable experiences. I believe that dropping out would have, in the long run, damaged my marriage.

I am continually amazed by the slowness with which the culture of expectation is changing. Conditioned attitudes are part of the problem, but I think there is something else that is less innocent. From the institution's point of view, those of us who cooperate willingly in the "two-person single career" model of academic leadership, who take up the tasks that leaders simply can't manage, are handy folks to have around. It may appear that the academy has a good deal going, and why, then, should the impetus for change come from that quarter? I would argue, however, that it could have an even better deal going, that institutions are not profiting as much as they might. The spouses are a talented group, and in many places their talents are being squandered on mundane things, their energy depleted by the exasperation they feel when their partners aren't provided with the support staff that is needed. Since the academy is the biggest loser when spouses drop out or never get involved in the first place, it might well start looking at how to keep them engaged.

Institutional Care for the Spouse. Some spouses love their situation, some are passably comfortable and others put up a good front. Some are, for career or family reasons or purely as a matter of choice, completely out of the picture. There will probably always be a mix of this sort. The spouse group is, as I said at the start, a very mixed bag. But boards of trustees need to realize that spouses can start out with friendly feelings toward the institution and end up exasperated, resentful, even hostile. That is not a healthy state of affairs for institution, leader or spouse. Surely boards would want to prevent this if at all possible, but I don't delude myself that it is a simple or easy task. Boards must be truly attentive to the spouses, as opposed to merely courteous; real effort is required. Spouses will not be openly candid in response to a casual "How's it going?" Like the leaders, they quickly learn to say what they think the constituent wants to hear. They will be more patient and trusting with interlocutors who can exhibit some understanding of the issues that spouses face.

Early intervention is always the best, and in this regard institutions can get off to a good start by developing a direct relationship with the spouse. In *The President's Spouse* David Riesman suggested that, when a new leader is coming from outside the institution, the search committee should work with the incoming spouse until after the leader has been installed, usually a period of some months. Alternatively, a special transition team might be given the responsibility of facilitating the induction of the spouse. I think that's a terrific idea; I wish I knew how to foster its implementation!

Spouses who are brand new to their roles should receive special attention. From the start they are one huge step behind. Their partners, the leadership candidates, become well-acquainted with the institution's history, its hopes and its needs during the interview stage. They develop a good understanding of what the job is going to entail. They have been building the requisite skills for years, if not decades. The spouses, on the other hand, have probably not been prepping themselves for the new life that now looms before them. Their personalities may suit them well for the role of leader's spouse—or perhaps not. As job candidates are interviewed their spouses may be kept on the sidelines, with little opportunity to learn about the institution and the job at hand. If the search committee brings them into the negotiations at all, it is usually in the final stages of the search.

I have often thought that trustees should offer to assign one of their body to act as a liaison to the spouse during the transition period, especially if he or she has no prior experience as the leader's spouse. Personally, I would have welcomed that sort of connection, especially if the trustee was someone who, through experience or study, had a good understanding of the impact of an academic leader's job on his or her family. A little sensitivity toward the spouse's unique situation and the sizeable adjustment that is involved would, I believe, go a long way toward keeping spouses engaged in positive ways.

[I am aware that there are several ways in which offering the spouse a special relationship with a trustee could backfire, particularly if the leader and spouse are not on the same page about the spouse's involvement, or if the marriage is already on the rocks. For that reason, it should probably be offered only after discussion with, and approval by, the incoming leader, and should be clearly described as a short-term relationship to provide support during the first year.]

Another way for the institution to get off to a good start with the spouse is to analyze what the leadership position might require in the way of support staff. Some institutions have begun to supply their leaders with extra support staff to help manage the residence and the entertaining, and they should be congratulated. But others are still leaning heavily on the spouses in these areas, perhaps not realizing it. When a married leader is set to retire or leave an institution, the trustees might ask that leader's spouse to list any tasks that he or she performed on the leader's behalf. These will generally be tasks that could just as easily be handled by hired staff. This exercise would highlight the areas where the institution might need to provide increased support to ensure that both office and residence function smoothly under the new administration. It is the only way I can think of to overcome the persistent problem of expectations being passed along from one spouse to another. It would also alert the board to the special plight of a new leader who does not have a spouse who is able or willing to task-share. Perhaps a house manager would be needed, to oversee the maintenance and frequent repairs that a larger, older residence might require. Perhaps an events manager should be provided, someone who will remember to notify the gardener ahead of time when an event is scheduled at the residence, someone who can be on the spot when the flowers or the folding tables or the bar supplies are delivered. A spouse who doesn't want to take on these responsibilities will benefit from this kind of help, as will a leader who has no one else to whom they can be delegated. From personal experience I can honestly say that having staff available to help keep matters at the official residence organized is priceless.

Spouse to Spouse. When I think of the many leaders' spouses I have met over the years, it strikes me that, as a group, we do not give ourselves much credit. The reason is, perhaps, not far to seek. We are a shadowy bunch, doing some of our best work out of sight, behind closed doors. Also, some of our work is, or soon becomes, second nature. It is tied to our marriage vows. The bottom line is that we are simply supporting the ones we love, and perhaps it strikes us as unseemly to congratulate ourselves for doing that. But I would argue that good spousework is hard-won and an effort in which we should all take pride.

If we who have already accrued some experience in the spouse role can begin to give ourselves a little more credit, benefit will accrue to those who are just entering this role. Spousework is complex and unsung; there is an art to doing it well, and it is an art which we all must teach ourselves. In the first chapter I used parenthood as an analogy to illustrate the depth and breadth of change that the new leader and his or her spouse experience. I return to that analogy here at the end. The pay-off for good parenting, as opposed to careless parenting, is huge. The same is true for spousework. The couple and the institutional community will recognize the difference it makes.

Partners of newly-appointed leaders need to know all this. They need to be supported in the early days so that they don't turn away in frustration and disappointment before even giving spousework a chance. Before the new leader takes up office, before the family moves into the official residence, these people need some preparation, some insight into the changes and challenges they are going to face. By and large, they are not getting it.

The National Association of Independent Schools and the Council of Independent Colleges are among a handful of organizations that are reaching out to spouses and helping them connect with one another. However, many of us are at institutions which do not belong to any national organization that recognizes spouse issues. While I laud those groups that show some concern for spouses, I feel that much more could, and perhaps should, be done, considering the impact that the leader's career has on his or her family.

What a delight it would be if a network of spouses was available to all of us. Is it too ambitious to suggest that there should be an organization for spouses alone, no matter what groups their institutions or their partners belong to—an organization that is designed primarily for us, rather than the academic leaders? Imagine typing "supportingspouses.org" on the computer and coming up with texts of a dozen discussions of mutual concerns, or better yet, the names of spouses around the country who are interested in networking. I think the time has come for something of that sort.

Society is largely ignorant of the way spouses contribute, the problems they tackle and the changes they accept. We are not the only group about which one could make such a statement, and I don't make it because I want to label us as suffering victims. But this is not a healthy situation for us, our partners or the academy. It is because of this lack of understanding that search committees and boards of trustees are making promises on which they cannot deliver. Spouses are not, and perhaps never can be, entirely free to behave as they like. They have implicit responsibilities toward their partners and the institutions their partners serve. And while, strictly speaking, they may be free to choose their own level of involvement, they might have to fight for the right to choose, over and over again.

In many places and in many ways the spouses of academic leaders are still expected to pour tea, and some of us continue to allow ourselves to be pressed into service. The era of "no expectations" will never come if the spouses sit and wait. Spouses need to make their institutions aware of the problem, if unwanted tasks are falling to them because there is no one else at hand. Somehow members of all constituencies should be given to understand that when we spouses are actively involved, whether it is planning events, caring for official residences, or standing in receiving lines, it is by our own choice—that we might at any time say "no" and do so with the board's blessing. There is some risk in this; we might be considered selfish, unpleasant, demanding, even unsupportive. But nothing risked, nothing gained. Our freedom to engage in spousework on our own terms will never be real until we make it so.

The Male Point of View: "It has been a long and largely mentor-less education for me. I think that I am a better husband in general, and definitely a better leader's support person than before ... I understand now more than ever that there is no way to know how to be the perfect partner to the president, but I am no longer afraid to embrace the scope of its possibilities."

978-0-595-45609-3
0-595-45609-X

Made in the USA
Lexington, KY
11 January 2010